INSIDE THE PRESIDENT'S TEAM

Family, Service, and the Gerald Ford Presidency

BOB BARRETT

PEGASUS BOOKS

NEW YORK LONDON

*The posthumous publication of this memoir is dedicated
in memory to its author, Robert E. Barrett*

—⊗—

INSIDE THE PRESIDENT'S TEAM

Pegasus Books, Ltd.
148 West 37th Street, 13th Floor
New York, NY 10018

First Pegasus Books cloth edition January 2025

Interior design by Maria Fernandez

Library of Congress Cataloging-in-Publication Data is available.

Hardcover ISBN: 978-1-63936-807-5
Ebook ISBN: 978-1-63936-808-2

10 9 8 7 6 5 4 3 2 1

Printed in the United States of America
Distributed by Simon & Schuster
www.pegasusbooks.com

Contents

Introduction

It was April 1978. I was sitting in Dr. Joe Pursch's small office with the former president and his wife. Betty Ford was preparing to be checked in for a four-week drug rehab program at the Long Beach Naval Hospital—the family had held an intervention a week earlier to address her addiction to opioids, originally prescribed over fifteen years earlier to alleviate pain from a pinched nerve. We all knew the drugs weren't the only addiction Mrs. Ford was battling, and perhaps not even the main one, but it had been hard enough on her and the family to confront the pain meds issue. Dr. Pursch, the family physician who had also been present at the family intervention, delicately offered her the opportunity to own up to her other demon.

"Well, Mrs. Ford, is there anything else you would like to tell us before going into the rehab program?" he asked.

"No," she said thoughtfully, as though she really was considering it. Here was a lady with tremendous self-control and dignity. The president sat quietly, looking from her to the doctor, in full support of the love of his life.

I knew what Dr. Pursch was after. In my four years with this impressive couple, I had watched her pour a large glass of vodka over ice at nine every morning and nurse it until four in the afternoon. She would then pour another that lasted until dinner, when the drinks began to flow more freely. Far too many nights I had seen her end the evening in an extreme state of intoxication.

"Are you sure?" Pursch persisted. "There's nothing else you need to tell me?"

"No, no. I can't think of anything," she said.

Her doctor was determined not to let it go. If he was going to encourage the former first lady of the United States to enter a rehab program, by God he wanted it to be effective.

"Please, Mrs. Ford. I need you to seriously consider this. Are you confident there's nothing else we need to address when you enter this program?"

Finally, she broke down.

"Well, maybe alcohol," she confessed through tears. "Maybe the booze."

She began to sob uncontrollably. In one of the tenderest moments I witnessed between these two, and there were many during the three decades I spent with them, the president reached over and gently held her hands. This man, who once held the most powerful position in the entire world, had lived with and loved an alcoholic for at least twenty years. As far as I knew, and I knew a lot, he had never confronted her about it. Seeing her break down and accept the truth, he began to cry as well.

"Goddammit, you two," the Boy Scout who rarely said a curse word said to the doctor and me, "she's said she's going in there. Now make it happen!"

What follows is the fractured fairy tale of a thirty-five-year-old US Army major who found himself invited to serve as the military aide to one sitting United States president, Richard Milhouse Nixon, and less than one month later began a two-and-a-half-decade-long relationship with the man who replaced him, and with his family. With five former wives in my rearview mirror, I'm probably not the man you want your son to model his family life after. But the person you will meet in these pages, Gerald Rudolph Ford Jr., should be. Jerry Ford was the most decent, honorable, trustworthy person I ever met. He was 98 percent koala bear and 2 percent grizzly, and he and his lovely, force-of-nature wife brought me into the orbit of their family and made me feel like a son. I committed to serving my country when I joined the army—I did that and so much more while serving the Fords.

1

Elephant in the Room

Tens Are Wild

It was not that long ago, though it seems like eons. A different world entirely. Two superpowers, the United States and the Soviet Union, with a third waiting in the wings—Communist China—ruled the Earth, all three with their fingers on the trigger of nuclear Armageddon. There were smart people, but no smartphones. There was interaction, intercourse, and international relations, but no Internet. My grandchildren may wonder: how did we ever survive? I look back sometimes and wonder the same thing.

The call came at exactly ten after ten in the morning, Wednesday, July 10, 1974. It was the third straight day of temperatures soaring into the high nineties—the kind of heat and humidity that comes down on you like a steam press, taking the starch out of you and your army-issued uniform. But that was no excuse. At the United States Army War College at Carlisle Barracks, we were all expected to straighten up and fly right, heat and humidity be damned.

I had been assigned to the college late in 1973 as the public affairs and communication officer, tasked with the job of getting word out about the place. The students here—the future leaders of the leading military power in the world—were getting the equivalent of a PhD and were destined to take teaching positions at West Point, to testify before Congress about billion-dollar budgets, or, if it came to it, to map out—and possibly execute—strategies for World War III. The powers that be in the US Army were justly proud of the program and wanted to get as much press coverage as they could—which is where I came in.

Getting called out of a meeting at Carlisle to take a phone call was highly unusual and disconcerting; such interruptions were simply not part of army protocol. Consequently, as I marched across the grassy quadrangle from Root Hall, where I had been meeting with some professors about a press release I was writing, to the main building, where the mysterious call waited in my office, I had to wonder if there had been a death in my family or if my house was on fire. Neither turned out to be the case. No, both my family and my house were intact. This was my country calling—and as I would discover in the coming weeks, it was my country that was on fire.

Answering the Call

W. L. "Bill" Gulley grew up dirt poor in America's heartland, rising out of the country's Great Depression to become a shining example of its Greatest Generation. Serving with the 1st Marine Division, he was wounded at Guadalcanal in World War II, won the Presidential Unit Citation in the Korean War, and was later deployed with Marine Air Group 14 to the Florida Keys during the Cuban Missile Crisis. Selected in 1966 to serve as chief administrator in the military aides office in the East Wing of the White House, he eventually rose to become director of the White House Military Office, exercising command and control of Air Force One, Marine One, Camp David, the White House Communications Agency, the military aides to the president, the White House Medical Unit, the White House bomb shelter, the White House garage, and the White House staff. In addition to all that, Bill Gulley was one rough, tough, gruff SOB—and that was who was waiting patiently on the other end of the line for me to pick up the phone.

Bill was not a man to waste words or his breath. He wanted to know if I was interested in being considered for nomination to the position of army aide to the president of the United States.

My first thought was: *Is somebody jerking my chain?* My second was: *One does not get called out of a meeting at the United States Army War College to have one's chain jerked.* My third: *Jesus Christ, I'm talking to the White House.*

I had no idea how or why my name came up as a candidate for the position. One did not seek the job; the job came looking for you. Clearly I had some expertise in the field of communications, and when working for the leader of the free world, knowing when to open your mouth and when to keep it shut, what to say and what to keep to yourself, and how to move mountains by making a few phone calls are all skills that can come in handy. But how my name worked its way up the military food chain was a complete mystery to me. And it wasn't a question I could ask.

I was just a soldier, and any insight into how these two behemoths of American power—the White House and Pentagon—ingested and digested all the data at their disposal, ultimately spitting out the name *Bob Barrett* as presidential-aide material, was above my pay grade. I didn't have a need to know. For the moment, the only communication Bill Gulley needed from me was a simple *yes* or simple *no.*

My heart was pounding, my head was spinning, and my stomach was churning. What was I supposed to do? In Vietnam I had commanded the 1st Battalion of the 73rd Field Artillery, requiring split-second life-and-death decision-making. But standing here at the phone, at attention, I was completely at sea. I knew that my life would be determined, from that moment on, by the answer I gave. I held my own fate in my own hands—and didn't know what the hell to do with it. I asked Gulley if I could have some time to think about it.

"Take all the time you want, Major Barrett," he said. "I'll need your answer at eleven." Forty-five minutes and counting.

No-brainer

With its tree-lined streets, car shows, and downtown movie marquee, Carlisle is a sweet, friendly apple-pie slice of small-town Americana. The Army War College, situated a few miles from the exact midpoint of the Appalachian Trail, is just far enough west, away from the madding crowds along the East Coast, to provide a quiet retreat—an incubator designed to advance military thinking, military strategy, and military careers.

I had enjoyed all the benefits of the college. I had been to Vietnam—to hell and back. Still, nothing could have prepared me for that phone call—and the choice that I had to make in the next forty-five minutes. I hung up and stared out the window at the barracks. The idea of leaving them unnerved me. I was thirty-five and comfortable in my skin and in my work. Life was good.

The choice was deceptively simple: Stay here, all but guaranteeing a bright, successful future—a steady rise through the army ranks. Or uproot my family for a future I couldn't even begin to imagine—pull out of this small-town Pennsylvania paradise and leap blindfolded into the Pennsylvania Avenue pressure cooker in Washington, DC. And not only that . . . it would mean scuttling my two-year assignment to the college and bailing on my boss, General Dewitt Smith, a two-star general.

I went to his office and said it was an emergency—I had to talk to him. He immediately put me at ease. With his kind face and gentle demeanor, General Smith had what I consider to be a fundamental quality of good leadership—the ability to empathize with those under his command.

"Sir," I said, standing in his office. "I've got a situation."

"Sit down, Major Barrett," he said. He walked around to his side of the desk and sat across from me. "What's on your mind?"

I laid it out for him—the call from Bill Gulley at the White House, the floating of the position as army aide to the president, and the short timeframe in which I had to make my decision. I expressed to General Smith my doubts about taking the job in the White House, tempered by my concern that it might be my duty to accept it.

The general shook his head; the situation as he saw it was quite the opposite. Gulley's phone call was just a bit of reconnaissance. There was a reason why he hadn't *ordered* me to take the job: If I didn't want it, he didn't want me to take it. It would be my duty to refuse. Smith then proceeded, slowly and deliberately, as I stole glances at my watch, the minutes ticking by, to tell me all the reasons *not* to pursue the position.

First of all, he pointed out, even if I accepted the offer, there was no guarantee that I would get the job. I had been invited to be *considered* to work for the president, and before passing muster, I would have to run through an obstacle course of interviews and interrogations. I'd have to "jump through hoops" was how General Smith put it—hoops thrown up by various personal and political aides to the president, as well as Secret Service agents, secretaries, and so on. If any one of them didn't like my answers—or didn't like the look on my face—I'd be cut loose and sent back to Carlisle without so much as a "Thank you very much."

And, General Smith went on, even if I did get the job—that would be no picnic either. He had spent some time in Washington, and he knew how brutal the place could be.

Like Caesar's wife, I would have to be above suspicion. The only reason there was a need at the moment for an army aide was because on a trip to the Middle East a few weeks before, during which President Nixon had met with Egyptian president Anwar Sadat, the previous aide was spotted drunk in a hotel bar. End of story: that man's military career was effectively killed and buried by one too many martinis. Did I really want to put myself in that position—where every move I made would be scrutinized, analyzed, and perhaps investigated? For me, the White House would be a glass house.

Smith didn't stop there but kept piling on. As the official US Army voice of the commander in chief, I would have to learn how to say *no* to men in the Pentagon who far outranked me. Some would try to curry favor with me to get close to the president. Others would simply resent me for enjoying the access they envied. But, then again, if I ever tried to take advantage of that access, I'd be out on my ear on Pennsylvania Avenue. The people around the president would guard their turf like tribal chieftains—and the moment I overstepped my bounds, the knives would come out.

So it went for forty-five minutes, General Smith drawing a picture of a spider's web of suspicion, intrigue, and sticky situations that no one in his right mind would volunteer to enter. I looked at my watch. Five minutes to target. I had to make the call. I thanked General Smith and stood to go.

"I hope I've been helpful," he said.

"Yes, sir." I nodded, digesting all he had said. I turned to leave.

"Major Barrett," he said, stopping me.

"Yes, sir?"

"Go," he said. "It's the chance of a lifetime. Don't pass it up."

Of course he was right. There had never been any doubt.

Power Trip

I had been in many helicopters before. In Vietnam, helicopters were like pigeons in Venice or taxicabs in Manhattan—they were all over the place, and the best way to get you where you were going. But this was something else. The big-bellied beast dropping out of the hot sky that afternoon—two and a half hours after I made the call—and landing on the Carlisle Barracks green was a flying fortress and conference room with cream-leather upholstered seating for sixteen, wood paneling, and a wet bar.

What was I doing in this monster helicopter? I could easily have hopped on a bus or commercial flight out of Harrisburg and made it to DC none the worse for wear. But that kind of thinking no longer applied. I was flying in a different airspace now and breathing different air. I was in the orbit of the commander in chief, entering a strange new world bound and determined by the dictates of executive privilege and power. I was headed into the land of the giants, and the Sea King was my first glimpse of the place.

As the helicopter scudded over the rolling hallowed ground of Gettysburg and across the fortieth parallel into Maryland, I sat on the edge of my seat, feeling like a kid—not in a candy store, but in a fragile multimillion-dollar flying machine belonging to the president of the United States. I folded my hands in my lap, careful not to move or touch anything for fear I would break it.

The helicopter touched down late that afternoon at Fort McNair, a US Army post located at the confluence of the Potomac and Anacostia Rivers in Washington, DC. As I stepped out of the air-conditioned comfort of the Sea King and onto the helipad, I discovered that, as far as the heat was concerned, Carlisle, Pennsylvania, had nothing on the nation's capital—which made the appearance of Sergeant Fred Ingersoll, White House driver, that much more remarkable.

In creased slacks, sharp gray blazer, and tie, the sergeant appeared as cool and crisp as his salute, not a drop of sweat on him. He took my bag, set it down in the trunk of the car, and opened the rear door for me. This was heady stuff for a kid from the working-class side of the South Shore of Long Island, but I just went along with the program—from the Sea King to the back seat of a chauffeur-driven White House car. Rarely am I at a loss for words, but on that fifteen-minute drive, all I could muster was something along the lines of *How about this heat?* A light rain had begun to fall—the kind that does not cool the air but merely dampens it.

My day had begun, with my usual 6:00 A.M. cup of black coffee, in the mess at Carlisle Barracks, but it had taken an incredible turn—leading me through the rain-slickened Washington streets, across the National Mall, within shouting distance of the Lincoln Memorial, Washington

Monument, and the dome of the United States Capitol. History was taking me for a ride, and I took in each point along the way with a degree of awe and dread. I knew where I came from, but not where I was going—I was having a hard time connecting the dots and getting my bearings.

Unconcerned with the NO PARKING sign out front, Ingersoll pulled up to the Hay-Adams hotel, the rain coming down more heavily now, took my bag, and led me through the front door, across the lobby, into the elevator, and up to my room. His duty done—his charge safely bivouacked for the night—the sergeant took his leave. Now what? I didn't know what to do, other than wait for my next cue. I pulled back the window curtains, and there it was, two minutes away, across Lafayette Park, hunkered down in the gloom of the falling rain and failing light of day. The White House.

Earlier, on the helicopter, I had sat on the edge of my seat. Now I did the same on the bed. I hadn't eaten since breakfast but was afraid to go out. What if I left the room and someone called? Couldn't risk that. And there was no way I was going to order room service. I imagined the president reading his credit card bill at the end of the month and asking, "Who's this goddamn guy ordering a cheeseburger and fries at the Hay-Adams?"

I'd eat, I told myself, when I got an order to eat, and not before. Sleep, however, seemed like a good idea. The sun had gone down, and so should I—rest up for whatever the hell was going to happen next. I lay down on top of the covers, careful not to muss the bed. Whose room *was* this? It sure didn't feel like mine.

Rough Country

That summer, 1974, the country was on edge.

A year and a half had passed since the signing of the Paris Peace Accords, signaling the end of the US military's direct involvement in the Vietnam

War. Still, as the South Vietnamese government and army—our allies in the war—slowly but surely collapsed, more and more Americans were asking whether the loss of more than 50,000 American lives had been in vain. Some thought we never should have been in Vietnam in the first place; others said we should have stuck it out and finished the job. But almost everyone came away from the experience with a powerful sense of distrust and doubt of our government that wasn't there a decade before.

Another war in another part of the world had also left America with a lingering hangover. In October 1973, Egypt and Syria—joined later by Jordan and a coalition of other Arab countries in the Middle East—launched a surprise attack on Israel. Besieged on all sides, Israel faced the possibility of choosing between total destruction or the use of its nuclear arsenal against its enemies. The United States government and its allies saw neither option as a viable one, and so began a massive rearmament of Israel, which helped turn the tide of the Yom Kippur War in its favor.

Peace came at a high cost. In retaliation for America's support of Israel, several Arab states, led by Saudi Arabia, declared an oil embargo, leading to an energy crisis here that sent the American economy reeling. The embargo ended in the spring of 1974 but left behind an anxious sense of vulnerability. The whole idea of America—of its ingenuity and invincibility—seemed to be running out of gas, as smaller countries that some had never heard of started pushing us around.

You couldn't turn on the evening news or open a newspaper that summer without sighing in frustration or fighting off an urge to punch a wall.

On Long Island, near where I grew up, a mysterious tide of sludge was creeping toward the beaches. Health officials declared that it was safe to swim but added that it would be beneficial to find new ways to dispose of sewage as the amount of human waste being dumped in the ocean increased.

In Boston, in an attempt to desegregate the public schools, a judge ordered that students be bused to schools outside of their own neighborhoods, Black kids sent to predominantly white schools and vice versa. The city responded with riots, mob violence, and racially inspired attacks on schoolchildren.

In California, a young woman named Patty Hearst—who had been kidnapped and radicalized by a violent self-styled revolutionary group calling itself the Symbionese Liberation Army—remained at large. Heir to one of the greatest fortunes ever amassed by an American publisher—her grandfather William Randolph Hearst—she had changed her name to Tania and had recently been photographed robbing a bank with an M1 carbine.

In movie theaters that summer, another innocent—a young girl named Regan played by Linda Blair—was possessed by a different kind of demon in *The Exorcist*. Viewers lined up around the block for the chance to see Regan curse at a priest and her mother, levitate off her bed, and rotate her head 360 degrees. In other films, a political reporter (Warren Beatty in *The Parallax View*) uncovered a massive conspiracy to assassinate public officials, only to end up a victim of it; and a cynical but well-meaning private detective (Jack Nicholson in *Chinatown*) discovered that nothing is what it seems, men of wealth and power can get away with anything—rape, incest, murder—and that massive cover-ups are business as usual.

These were the stories Americans wanted to hear—stories that confirmed their worst fears about the souls of their children and of their ruling class. Even as they took off on vacation, heading for the beaches, they took along a book (*Jaws*) that warned them of the dangers lurking just beneath the surface of the water. Swim at your own risk.

It was the summer of anxiety, paranoia, and dark doings—the gloom spreading from the White House across the country. And I was by no means immune to the sense of tension and foreboding. I swam in the same murky, shark-infested waters as the rest of the country—and, if anything, I was being drawn deeper into it.

Retreat

It was 8:00 A.M., July 11, 1974, at the Hay-Adams hotel. I had already been up for four hours, and the first thing I had done earlier that morning was put in a call to my wife, Bev, back in Carlisle. We had been high school sweethearts and had gotten married in 1960. While I ended up in the army, she got a degree in education and went on to teach elementary school students. Bev has the patience of a saint, evidenced not only by her choice of career, but by the fact that she was still married to me after fourteen years.

My phone call woke her up, and I told her exactly what I knew about my situation—which was exactly nothing. But it was good to hear her familiar calm, reassuring voice. We couldn't talk more than a few minutes—it was long distance, and I didn't know who was paying for it—so I hung up and waited. The call came from Bill Gulley, at eight on the dot, from the White House. Although it was no more than a few football fields' length from where I sat, I wasn't going there today. He told me a car was coming to take me to Andrews Air Force Base.

The heat wave had broken overnight, and Washington shimmered in the clear morning air. But I wouldn't be around to enjoy it. I was headed some three thousand miles to the west: to San Clemente, on the opposite coast.

Lee Simmons was a gentleman's gentleman. A member of the US Air Force since the early 1950s, he had served in the 89th Air Force squadron—the presidential air fleet—under every president from Eisenhower on. Within a decade, in the Kennedy administration, he became the first African American to fly as a crew member on Air Force One—a position that, back in the early 1960s, must have required a Jackie Robinson–like degree of courage and self-control. On trips to some cities in the South, he had to eat in different restaurants and sleep in different hotels from the rest of the plane's crew.

By the time I met Lee that morning at Andrews Air Force Base, when I boarded the Lockheed JetStar—a smaller executive jet in the presidential fleet that would fly me out to California—he had risen to the position of personal steward to President and Mrs. Nixon. But neither of them was flying on this day, so he was assigned the task of stewarding me across the country. The first thing Lee asked me as we took off from Andrews was what I wanted for lunch.

I'm a wise guy by nature, and any other time I would have cracked wise. But this wasn't any other time. I had left that guy back in Carlisle. On any military flight I'd ever been on, you ate what you were served, and even on a large commercial flight, you usually had two choices: the baked chicken or the Salisbury steak. And this was a small jet—there couldn't have been *that* much of a choice.

"What do you have?" was my perfectly logical response. I'd have been grateful for a ham sandwich.

Lee narrowed his eyes in thought. "You look like a steak man to me," he said. I must have agreed with his assessment, as twenty minutes later a meal appeared before me—a thick Porterhouse steak, baked potato, creamed spinach, and a fresh salad—worthy of a Midtown Manhattan steak house. Ascertaining that I was "between assignments" and not technically on duty, Lee brought out a glass of red wine to go along with my lunch.

It was beginning to dawn on me that, as a member of the US military in the direct service of the president, I would be the conduit of an awesome amount of power and responsibility. Yes, it was *just* a steak, but it was *just* a helicopter that had picked me up in Carlisle, it was *just* a hotel room I had stayed in last night, and this was *just* a presidential jet carrying me from sea to shining sea.

If I were to become the US Army aide to the president, and he were to order a steak for lunch or an aircraft carrier on which to entertain a foreign dignitary, I would, as often as not, be the one to make the call. I would be like the genie let out of the military bottle, able to grant the president's every wish. And there would be one genie you hoped never to have to let out of the bottle: I would be the man at the president's side carrying "the football"—the briefcase that I would open and hand over to the commander in chief in the event of a nuclear attack on the United States.

A dizzying thought. But I tried to put it aside, relax, and enjoy the flight. It was a nice steak, after all, and very good wine.

President Nixon put San Clemente, California, on the map. Prior to his purchase of an estate there, on a bluff overlooking the Pacific Ocean, the area was known only for attracting swallows to the nearby Mission San Juan Capistrano and surfers to the beaches. To everyone else the place was just a sign on Interstate 5 about halfway between Los Angeles and San Diego. That all changed in 1969 when Nixon bought the ten-room Spanish-style California Mission Revival mansion as a place to escape the Sturm und Drang of Washington, DC. He dubbed the house *La Casa Pacifica*—the House of Peace. Everyone else called it the Western White House.

Japanese prime minister Eisaku Sato, South Vietnamese president Nguyen Van Thieu, and Soviet leader Leonid Brezhnev had all had their time in the sun at the Western White House, and now I would have mine.

The JetStar landed at Marine Corps Air Station El Toro, an enormous air base since decommissioned, about a forty-five-minute drive from San Clemente. A Secret Service agent and yet another car were waiting for me. The agent put a pin on my lapel, handed me the keys, and gave me the address of a hotel on Interstate 5. No driver this time—I was on my own. After one night in the hotel acclimating to my changing circumstances—I ordered dinner and charged it to my room, made long-distance phone calls at will, and slept under the covers—I got the call. Friday, July 12, I was headed for the House of Peace.

I pulled up to the entrance of the Western White House, and the sergeant on guard there took one look at the pin on my lapel, and I was in like Flint, a member of the secret club. He pressed a button and opened the gate.

"Good morning, Major Barrett," he said.

And the last thing I remember doing with any confidence was saying good morning back. I glanced into the rearview mirror, the gate closing behind me, and, as warm as it was in that Southern California sunshine, felt a chill. I had crossed the Rubicon.

They say in San Clemente that on a clear day you can see forever, but on that day, there was no clarity whatsoever. I reported to the office of the deputy assistant to the president for national security affairs, Major General Brent Scowcroft. Small, quiet, unassuming, and razor-sharp, Scowcroft was at the time, perhaps, the most powerful man in the US military. Here was a guy who had the ear—and the respect—not only of Nixon, but of National Security Advisor and Secretary of State Henry Kissinger, as well as White House Chief of Staff Alexander Haig. No small feat considering the Olympic-sized egos of those three men.

Scowcroft was polite but to the point. He clearly had more pressing matters to deal with that morning than me. He dispatched me to go grab some lunch and promptly forgot about me.

I quickly came to the conclusion that everybody in the Western White House had more pressing matters to deal with that morning. I sat in the mess, alone, for four hours consuming nothing but time. When I left Carlisle I had been told, as I was between assignments, to leave my uniforms behind. In other words, I was up in the air. As a result, sitting there in the lunchroom in my civilian clothes, the executive branch of the US government coming and going and buzzing around me, I felt all out of sorts, out of place, and out of time—with nothing to ground me other than a pin on my lapel.

I was a soldier without a uniform, an aide without a commander, a man without a clue as to what I was supposed to do. But I wasn't alone. There was an eerie air of distraction about this place, haggard looks on people's faces—everyone in a kind of limbo. And with good reason. There was an elephant in the room. The government that summer was grinding to a halt, the presidency collapsing and sucking the energy out of everyone.

There was no precedent for what was happening, no way for any of us to measure the degree of danger we were in. It wasn't just that the people around the president feared that they might lose their jobs—they feared that they might lose their country.

July 10, the day I left the comfortable, insulated confines of Carlisle for the nation's capital, the headline in the *Washington Post* had been: TRANSCRIPTS LINK NIXON TO COVER-UP.

July 11, the day I flew west—enjoying that Porterhouse on the JetStar—the president's chief defense lawyer, James D. St. Clair, sought to discredit former White House counsel John Dean III. Committee members called Dean's testimony "hurtful" to Nixon and "a real bloodletting."

July 12, the day I arrived in San Clemente, Air Force One, with President Nixon aboard, landed at El Toro. He was bound for the Western White House. He was in retreat.

Blood was in the water. Sharks were circling.

The elephant in the room was Watergate.

By the time I found myself, in the summer of 1974, having lunch in the mess in the Western White House, the word *Watergate* had become a part of the American vernacular—as fraught with meaning as *Pearl Harbor, Hiroshima*, or *Lee Harvey Oswald*. From London to Moscow, from Beijing to Boise, everyone knew about *Watergate*—not the upscale complex of buildings on the banks of the Potomac, but the scandal that had turned 1600 Pennsylvania Avenue into a house of political trauma.

I grew up in the 1940s and 1950s, but, as I will show several chapters on, it was the 1960s that shaped my life and my future. It was a divisive, dangerous, deadly decade, pitting men against women, White people against Black people, students against teachers, and children against parents. Young men were burning their draft cards, young women were burning their bras, and nobody, it seemed, was getting any satisfaction.

It was in the midst of this fevered and thrashing chaos that Richard M. Nixon, in November 1968, was elected president, with considerably less than 50 percent of the vote and less than 1 percent over his Democratic opponent, Hubert Humphrey.

Gaining entry to the White House by a whisker, Nixon's team immediately began plotting strategy for the next presidential race—four years later in 1972. The fire in their bellies was fueled by two factors: 1) determination to take a second term by storm, avoiding another razor-thin election and, 2) lingering suspicions that, in Nixon's first run for the office in 1960, the presidency had been stolen from him by the Kennedy family. Not again. Nixon was going to win big by whatever means necessary. And his team succeeded. Quietly and anonymously plotting behind the scenes, they ultimately pulverized the Democratic candidate, George McGovern, with over 60 percent of the vote. It was a landslide, but it came on a slippery slope.

The bungled burglary at the Watergate was the loose thread that led to the ultimate unraveling of the Nixon presidency. Breaking and entering was just the beginning. Money laundering through Mexico. Secret slush funds used to spy on the opposition. Political dirty tricks. Trading influence for campaign contributions. Using the power of the executive branch—the FBI, CIA, and IRS—as a weapon against Nixon's enemies.

Did Nixon have enemies? Absolutely. Watergate was all that sixties shit—assassinations, Cuba, Vietnam, the decade of *us against them*— hitting the fan. Did Nixon's administration do anything that previous ones hadn't? Certainly other presidents had lied, sold influence, and abused their power—but the extent and degree of the abuses that Nixon allowed in that increasingly hostile environment was historic. In their obsession to bury the opposition, Nixon and his political operatives dug their own graves.

By the summer of 1974, people far more knowledgeable than I knew that the Nixon presidency was about to explode. And I had landed in the middle of it.

Another Day at the Office

The Southern California summer can lull you to sleep. Highs in the eighties, sunshine, zero percent chance of precipitation. It's like that movie with my golfing buddy Bill Murray, *Groundhog Day*—morning after morning, you wake up to the same déjà vu world of dry heat and blue skies. You forget all about the weather . . . until it hits. We were in San Clemente for two and a half weeks. It rained once, ten days into our stay. But when the rain came, it came with a vengeance: thick, ominous clouds rolling in off the Pacific, the coast going dark at noon, rivers of water running down the streets, into the canyons, and back toward the ocean from where it came. The sky was falling. And the political torrent would pick up in the coming weeks.

Friday, July 12, the day I arrived in San Clemente, John Ehrlichman, President Nixon's former chief domestic advisor, was found guilty of conspiracy and perjury in the burglary of a psychiatrist's office in an attempt to dig up dirt on Daniel Ellsberg, who had released the Pentagon Papers.

Monday, July 15, Charles Colson, the president's former special counsel, testified before the House Judiciary Committee that Nixon approved the operation to break into the psychiatrist's office.

Friday, July 19, the two senior counsels to the Judiciary Committee urged the committee to recommend a Senate trial of the president.

Tuesday, July 23, the same day that the deluge hit San Clemente, Lawrence J. Hogan, a conservative Republican member of the committee, came out in favor of impeachment.

Wednesday, July 24, the Supreme Court voted 8 to 0 that the president must surrender the tapes—recordings of Nixon's meetings in the Oval Office, which would reveal what he knew about the Watergate cover-up and when he knew about it.

Saturday, July 27, the House panel voted 27 to 11 asking for the impeachment of the president for obstruction of justice.

It was surreal. Not more than a hundred yards from where I took my morning walks or read my morning papers, sat the man around whom these stories swirled—events unfolding out of his control, old friends and colleagues indicted and convicted, his own fate hanging in the balance. Here I was, at ease, out of uniform and if not on vacation, certainly not gainfully employed, sitting in sunny Southern California, in the eye of the storm, as the office of the United States presidency—arguably the most powerful institution in the world—was slowly, but with increasing velocity, coming apart at the seams.

The Mess

You've got to hand it to the US Navy. Nothing against the army, but when it comes to food, of the four branches of the military, the navy wins that war hands down. Maybe it's those long stretches at sea, the cooks having nothing better to do than hang around the galley honing their craft. Not surprisingly, the navy ran the White House kitchen, and its chief steward—the maestro of the mess—was Ron Jackson. At San Clemente, the mess opened for lunch at 11:30, and I was there at 11:31—not just for the food, but for the change of scenery. Alone with my thoughts and a damn good meal, I sat picking at the food, trying to make it last, mostly trying to eat away the hours. This time at San Clemente was my own long stretch at sea.

No one was going to sit with me, and I didn't blame them. They all knew the president—their boss—was in trouble, but none knew what it meant. Anxiety and uncertainty hung in the air and showed in people's eyes. It was spreading like a flu bug, and when something like that's going around, everyone's going to stay close to the people they know and trust. This was neither the time nor the place to make new friends. Those who were close to the president, or had been working for him for a long time, were on edge—raw and vulnerable and mistrustful of outsiders.

I was the new guy—an unknown quantity with no specified role—sitting alone at lunch. Who was I? What was I doing there? Whose side was I on? I had to walk a razor-thin line. I couldn't appear indifferent to the situation, nor could I seem too ambitious. If I tried to curry favor with civilian members of the staff, memos would be written and my ticket most likely punched—back to Carlisle. I couldn't be pro-Nixon, be anti-Nixon, or try to rise above the fray. Watergate did that, especially to many of us in the military—it intellectually emasculated us. I had to hunker down, button up, and keep my own counsel, hoping not to get hit by any stray bullets.

Running the Show

Just after lunch on my first full day in San Clemente, a member of the military staff took me around the compound, from one building to the next, introducing me to various people I might encounter during my time there. I knew this was not a mere formality. Once introduced, I would be expected to know and memorize the name, face, and role of each person I encountered, a task requiring focus, fluency, and a certain amount of grace under pressure—all of which, at one point, standing in a hallway with a group of three or four people, I lost entirely.

To this day, I don't remember what I was thinking or whose hand I was shaking when my concentration was broken. Our group of three or four had suddenly and without warning become a group of seven or eight, and at its center stood President Nixon. I'm sure from his perspective it was a completely unremarkable event: he had emerged from some meeting, seen an unfamiliar face being introduced around, and felt it incumbent upon himself to join the reception line. If I was here, I must work for him, and like any good boss—especially a political one—he put out his hand.

From my perspective, however, it was about as remarkable an event as I could imagine. It's not every day you meet the leader of the free world, and my heart rate was off the charts. I had to conjure up all my military discipline to clear my head, recover my focus, and deliver a signal from my brain to my hand to lift it up and shake his.

The president seemed a bit unsteady on his feet. I knew he had a history of phlebitis; what I didn't know at the time was that the condition had recently flared up. Nixon's doctors, fearing that a clot might break free—a potentially fatal complication—advised him to stay off his feet. The president ignored them; in June he had undertaken a grueling trip to the Middle East, standing for hours, waving to cheering crowds in Syria, Israel, and Egypt. It must have been worth risking death to soak up the adoration, even if it was in Cairo rather than in New York.

Our handshake was as stiff and short as our meeting. Not that he was rude or dismissive of me; he was simply abrupt. Nixon was a man of stark contrasts: a brilliant strategic mind, at ease on the world stage, who at the same time was socially insecure and uncomfortable in his own skin. No one becomes president without possessing absolute confidence in his own abilities, actions, and instincts. Which explains why *this* president might have confused the national interest with his own self-interest.

Of all the people I've ever come across in my life, and that includes politicians, soldiers, movie stars, and a whole lot of assholes, Richard Nixon was the most socially inept person I ever met. He didn't seem capable of speaking truth with an emphasis that made you believe him. His sense of humor was awkward and evidenced by a guttural laugh.

While we were in San Clemente, Jack Brennan, the loyal marine aide who stayed with Nixon after he left office, showed me a medal that Nixon was to present. To simplify his pinning the medal on the soldier, they had changed the clasp that held the pin to a large washer that replaced the circular ring normally used.

When the time came for the presentation, Nixon read out the written reason the soldier was receiving the reward in his flat, unemotional affect, went to pin on the medal, but still mishandled the clasp. The medal started sliding down the soldier's chest. Nixon slapped it hard against the soldier, and in his deep, coarse way of speaking, made a half-assed attempt at apologizing. It was obvious that he didn't know how to talk to blue-collar Americans, religious Americans, or so many of the citizens who had helped to elect him as president of the United States. It's amazing to me that he made it to where he did as a politician.

As they say, "All politics is local." You would probably have to look at what was going on when Nixon began his rise in politics in California to see what kind of rolling crescendo kept him in the mix and allowed for his ascendency—obtaining a place in Congress or a plum committee assignment. There were so many throws of the dice that allowed him an ongoing rise to power and position.

Nixon's conviction that he was good for the country—his résumé included détente with the Soviet Union and China, the creation of the Environmental Protection Agency, and putting America on the moon—must have created in Nixon's mind the antithetical notion that those who would depose him were bad for the country. That being the case, he would feel justified in retaining the presidency by whatever means necessary. Ironically, it was that certainty that led to Watergate—and Watergate that ultimately sapped him of the ability to lead. Now, limping over to shake my hand, he barely seemed in command of himself, let alone the country.

But the government was not rudderless. Like nature, power abhors a vacuum, and the man standing at the president's side was also the man behind the curtain.

With his rugged good looks, furrowed brow, hooded eyes, and disarming smile, General Alexander Haig came straight out of central casting. He looked equally sharp in military uniform and a Savile Row suit, and he played both parts—soldier and civil servant—with authority and aplomb. It was a role he seemed born for. During the Korean War, Haig served on the staff of General Douglas MacArthur in Japan, but it was a decade later, in

Vietnam, that he made his bones. It was a war that fit his ambitions, and, rising to the occasion, he quickly rose through the ranks.

I knew of Haig from my first tour of duty in Vietnam. Before I arrived in Vietnam, Lieutenant Colonel Haig was the G3, in charge of operations for the 1st Infantry Division (the Big Red One). He was not a man given to modesty, and he could never be accused of playing down his accomplishments in Vietnam—as reflected by the fruit salad of medals and ribbons displayed on his chest. As a military man, he was a skilled politician and had a reputation as a finagler and self-promoter—a certain amount of which is healthy in any career—and thoroughly enjoyed presenting himself as an insider, with unique access to those in power. Now, as chief of staff to a diminished president, General Haig was about as *inside* as he could get. And all the qualities that put him there—his fundamental understanding of how bureaucracy worked and how to get things done—served him, and the country, well.

The strain of running the day-to-day business of the government showed, however. In all those weeks, I don't think I ever saw the general without a cigarette in hand. It was understandable. He was guiding a hamstrung president, his lawyers, and his staff through the greatest constitutional challenge since the Civil War. All his talents and character traits, good and bad, weren't going to allow him to solve the unbelievable problems before him. The situation had become toxic.

Sideshow

With the president in San Clemente, every hotel, motel, and bed-and-breakfast within a five-mile radius was overrun (as was every bar and grill from five o'clock on). I was one small part of an occupying army: support staff, Secret Service, military details, and that other unruly horde—the press. Under normal circumstances the White House press corps was substantial; but now, with the president on a collision course with history, the reporters stepped away from their typewriters, strapped on their expense accounts, and descended on San Clemente. No one wanted to miss the crash.

Keeping the press at bay is like herding cats, which was why, for the most part, they were barred from the grounds of the Western White House. But one afternoon, out on one of my time-killing walks, I noticed a large gathering on the front lawn of the residence. Members of the press were viewed as barbarians by the Nixon camp, but the reporters, photographers, network cameramen, and soundmen had breached the gates and been allowed into the palace. All morning there had been a sense of heightened activity, the hive buzzing. Something was up. But if nobody volunteered to tell me what was going on, I was in no position to ask. Now, hanging back some distance away, I could find out for myself what the ruckus was all about.

Shortly, the president emerged from the front door of his residence followed closely by a second man. I couldn't get a good look at him, but I knew right away who he was. I'd seen him on television a few times without forming much of an impression: the vice president, Gerald Ford. Seeing him in person I was struck by his stature. He was a taller man than I had thought. His height might have been accentuated by the contrast between him and President Nixon, stooped at the shoulders, the weight of the world on his back.

The short press conference and photo op over—the president and vice president shaking hands—their staffs shepherded the two men away and out of sight. The press dispersed and headed out to reoccupy the saloons. It was nearly time for me to join them.

As I did at the end of every day, about 4:30, I headed in to check in, or rather check out, with Bill Gulley.

"Anything else I can do for you, sir?" I'd say, and he'd chuckle, both of us in on the joke that I hadn't done anything up to that point, and there was no reason to think that would change. Further, he never expected to be addressed as *sir*. He'd release me for the day, and I'd head back to my motel room, where I'd dial up my wife to tell her all the things I didn't do that day. She was as much in limbo as I was, not knowing our next move or where the kids—Nils, eight, and Kristy, six—would be going to school that fall. Married to the army, she was used to change. She'd put the kids on for a quick word, and they'd ask when I was coming home. Soon, I'd say, which was all they needed to hear. The catch was, I didn't know when or exactly where *home* was now.

On July 27, I had some actual news to share with my wife. The following day, I'd be heading east—not to Pennsylvania, but back to Washington. I'd be spending August in the urban swamplands of the nation's capital.

The White House was on the move—and I had become a part of it.

Up in the Air

For many of Nixon's people heading back to Washington, the departure from San Clemente was a difficult one: Their goodbyes to those staying behind at the Western White House were drawn out and emotional. There was a sense of finality about it—of mourning a loss. Being in limbo, without agenda or attachment, I was not so affected. But as they saw it, their president might still be breathing, but he was on life support, suffering a death by a thousand cuts, and they were all bleeding out with him.

Air Force One, with the president, his family, and top staff, had taken off hours before the rest of us boarded our plane to follow in his wake. The somber mood of the San Clemente farewell lingered in the cabin on the flight across the country. An oppressive mix of sadness, anger, and suspicion hung in the air. Those who had worked for—and believed in—Nixon for years were losing their faith, their confidence, and their direction.

I had a very brief conversation with my future boss during that flight. I was a bit shocked that the vice president of the United States would even take notice of me at that point in the evaluation process. I think Vice

President Ford had picked up on the fact that I was wondering how long I would be in limbo about the job.

"He's not in good shape, Bob," the vice president said, speaking of Nixon. "He's kind of hard to talk to right now. Of course, it's understandable that he's bitter about all this."

Stories had begun appearing in the papers about infighting and disarray on the White House staff. An angry General Haig had ripped into some members of the staff about those leaks—though it was rumored that Haig himself was one of the most active unnamed sources in all of Washington. Whatever the case, and whoever was responsible, this was a leaking ship—and a leaking ship is a sinking ship.

As the situation deteriorated, I had two things going for me: my ignorance and my anonymity. I didn't know a damn thing, and nobody knew who the hell I was. Those two qualities would serve me well over the next several weeks.

In a place like Washington, where facts, rumors, innuendo, and information are all served up with equal relish, not knowing something can at times be a great advantage. Nixon himself would have benefited from a little more ignorance—and a little less hubris. After all, *What did he know, and when did he know it?* was the question that ultimately scuttled his presidency.

Getting Grounded

My new digs were in the Bachelor Officer's Quarters at Bolling Air Force Base, in southwest DC, across the Potomac from what was then the Washington—now the Ronald Reagan Washington—National Airport in Virginia. It wasn't exactly the Hay-Adams, but that was fine. I felt more at ease here. I preferred austere. There was a twin bed, a couple of chairs, a television, and a table next to the bed with a telephone on it.

I stowed my stuff in the small closet and fell back on the bed. It was late, well after midnight, but my eyes were wide open—I was still on California time. Time to reflect. I took a deep breath and tried to take it all in: where I'd been, where I was now, and where I was going. But then I noticed something odd about the phone on the table next to me: it had no dial, no buttons, no numbers at all. Curious, I picked up the receiver.

"Yes, Major Barrett?"

"Sorry," I mumbled and hung up. Two o'clock in the morning and some disembodied voice out there is waiting patiently for me to pick up the phone? It scared the bejesus out of me. I took a closer look: on the small disk in the middle of the phone, where one would usually see the phone number, there was instead a tiny blue icon: the White House. I had been wired into a net that I didn't know existed—but, even more surprisingly, a net that knew of my existence. I was connected, the phone my umbilical cord. On the other end: the White House.

How many Americans, that morning of Monday, July 29, 1974, got out of bed, dragged a comb across their head, and took off for work? Millions, and I was one of them. But I felt like one in a million. My commute that day gave me gooseflesh and butterflies and made my head spin—just about every symptom of stress, anxiety, and stage fright imaginable. My destination, coming up on my right as I passed the Ellipse, was the White House. The *Holy shits!* just kept on coming.

I parked the car, walked to the gate, showed the guard my credentials, and in I went—not looking back this time, focused not on where I was coming from but on where I was going. I entered the East Wing and headed upstairs to the second floor to the Military Office, adjacent to the offices assigned to the first lady.

Many have claimed that the White House is haunted, and I have to agree—the place is an old ghosts' home. Jefferson, Jackson, Lincoln, a couple of Roosevelts, Eisenhower, and Kennedy, to name a few. They all ate here, slept here, made love and war here. And now, this office had a plain walnut desk with a lamp, a phone, and Bob Barrett's name on it. It was a heady, humbling, unnerving experience—and I loved it.

I was, at long last, beginning to understand what my job was: watch and learn. Maybe I *did* belong here. Sure, in the back of my mind I still had doubts. *Who did I think I was? What did I know? Who was I kidding?* So I did what any good soldier would do—I told the back of my mind to shut the hell up. Because we were all standing on the same ground—a ground riddled with fault lines—and the only thing any of us knew for certain was that there was no certainty to be had. Best not to think too much.

In the Military Office of the White House, a certain amount of intelligence and street smarts is a plus; but an excess of commentary on political process can do more harm than good. There were phones to answer, memos to type, and helicopter takeoffs and landings to arrange. Predicting how things might shake out in the next few days or weeks was like trying to piece together a puzzle of a million parts without knowing what the finished picture is supposed to look like. Leave that to the Henry Kissingers and Alexander Haigs to work out. It was their puzzle—we were just pieces of it trying to figure out where we fit, if at all.

Whenever I started to think how tough I had it, living with the uncertainty, I thought about the president or vice president and what they must be going through. My problems were a nervous tic compared to the monumental strains they must be under. The fact was: everyone in this place, from the Oval Office to the janitor's closet, had one thing in common: we were all, each and every one of us, totally confused. It was strangely reassuring.

Fault Lines

My wife was a different story. As an army spouse, Bev knew that putting down roots was a risky proposition: you could be yanked up at any moment and sent packing anywhere—from Guam to Guantanamo Bay. She was used to living in suspended animation, not knowing where my next assignment would take us, and had become quite good at it—exercising command and control over a household that, in the last eight years, had moved from Fort Sill, Oklahoma, to Upstate New York to Long Island to Fort Leavenworth, Kansas, to Carlisle, Pennsylvania. But my current situation, as muddied and muddled as it was, gave her pause.

The evening of Wednesday, July 31, instead of heading back to my quarters at Bolling after work, I took off north toward Carlisle, breaking a few speed limit laws along the way. I made the three-hour drive in two and a half, arriving a little after 8:30. Nils and Kristy were still up, a special night, Daddy coming home, and after some hugs, they settled down on the floor to watch TV before going to bed. Bev made me something to eat, and we sat and talked. She was neither angry nor anxious. She simply sought some clarity. But I had none to offer.

I told her to get ready for our next move—to Washington.

So that meant I had been offered the position at the White House?

Well, not exactly. Technically, no position had been offered.

When, then, would we be moving?

Soon, I assured her.

Where would we be living?

Someplace nice.

I would have been better off giving Bev my name, rank, and serial number and leaving it at that. She could live with uncertainty, but I was asking her to commit to a situation bordering on insanity. And she did, agreeing to prepare for the move and await my call. Looking back, though, I wonder if she intuited that I was more anxious to get back to the White House than I was to take the time and effort required to bring a sense of stability to *her* house.

Bev was the patient one, not me, and I had come to realize just how much I wanted the job in Washington. I craved the action and hyperactivity, the buzz that surrounds serving those in power; even the chaos of it appealed to me. I wanted to work among those White House ghosts.

After a few hours of sleep, I got up at three in the morning, kissed Bev and the sleeping kids goodbye, and hit the road, heading back to my future and to that phone with the little icon of the White House on it. Perhaps my impatience—my need to get away and get back to DC—exposed some tiny fissures in our marriage. If so, consciously or unconsciously, I chose to ignore them.

I loved my family and loved seeing them, but the real reason I had come back to Carlisle was to pick up my uniforms. I had to suit up for the game. I know that now but wouldn't admit it back then.

Thursday night, August 1, President Nixon was on the move, and I was moving with him. After three weeks in civvies, I put on the green jacket with the brass buttons. It felt good. It felt right. It felt like I belonged here.

Water under the Bridge

A presidential motorcade is a miraculous thing—as seamless as a jazz riff and as precise as a production of *Swan Lake*. The Secret Service choreographs the entire show, and if you're one of the players—as I was for the first time that Thursday evening—you just do as you're told, hit your marks, and go. Doors open and doors close, cars move through streets cleared of traffic and traffic laws, cars stop, doors open and close again, and you're there. You know you've gotten from point A to point B, you're just not quite sure how. It's all a blur. Where the blur took us that evening was to the Washington Navy Yard. The president was setting sail on the presidential yacht, the USS *Sequoia*—a quiet journey, away from his lawyers and advisors, down the Potomac to Mount Vernon, home of the first president, George Washington. Charles "Bebe" Rebozo was joining him on board for dinner.

The son of Cuban immigrants, Rebozo was a businessman and banker from Key Biscayne, Florida. He first met Nixon, then the newly elected senator from California, in 1950 and offered to take him out on a fishing trip. Rebozo's first impression of the future president was not a positive one. He described Nixon as "a guy who doesn't know how to talk, doesn't drink, doesn't smoke, doesn't chase women, doesn't know how to play golf, doesn't know how to play tennis, he can't even fish."

But there is as little logic to a good friendship as there is to a good marriage. (I have more experience of the former than the latter.) Despite that inauspicious start, over the next two decades—through Nixon's vice presidency under Eisenhower, his loss to Kennedy in 1960, his self-imposed exile from politics, and finally his triumphant return in 1968—Rebozo became one of his closest friends, confidants, and business advisors.

Appearing more and more like a helpless giant, Nixon stood on the brink of an awful choice: between impeachment by the US Senate and resignation—a self-imposed internal exile. It was no wonder, then, as the sword of Damocles hung over his head, that he would retreat to this yacht he loved with the one man he trusted. For if he gave up the presidency, Nixon would be giving up a world. The helicopters and jets and stewards and chefs and motorcades and brass bands . . . and the greatest piece of public housing imaginable—the White House. And this floating White House, the boat he loved.

Built in 1925, the USS *Sequoia* had been used by every president since. FDR plotted war strategy on board with then-general Eisenhower. Truman installed and played a piano in its main salon. Navy veteran John Kennedy socialized and ultimately celebrated his final birthday on the yacht. Nixon himself negotiated the first arms treaty with the Soviet Union on it. And now, on this lovely warm August evening, he returned to the *Sequoia* to decide whether to walk away from it—and all the other trappings of power. He was an emperor on the verge of stripping himself of his empire, and he must have seen Rebozo as the one man in his circle without a political agenda—someone who would be waiting for him on the other side.

Rebozo, however, *did* have an agenda. He was not simply there as the president's friend; he was also acting as an agent of the president's men. As Nixon lost his grip on the levers of power, was he also losing his grip on reality? Was he suffering from depression? Was it debilitating? Was he a desperate man capable of desperate acts? Did the country have to be protected from its own president? Did the president have to be protected from himself? Both presumptuous and pertinent, these questions needed answers. That was the fool's errand that brought Rebozo to the *Sequoia* that evening. The banker and businessman from Key Biscayne had been asked to act as psychiatrist, spy, witness, judge, and defender of the homeland. It was a strange time in American governance.

I sat on the yacht that day with Lieutenant Colonel Jack Brennan—the man I had been brought in possibly to replace. We were about thirty feet away from Nixon and Rebozo as they talked. While I couldn't hear specific words, I could hear their inflections, their tonality, the firmness with which they spoke, and the first suggestions of anger. Trying hard not to bring attention to myself, I occasionally glanced over Jack's shoulder to observe their facial expressions and body language.

While the president was being scrutinized by his friend Bebe, I was undergoing a similar, though far less significant, examination by Brennan. Although there had been no formal interviews for the position of army aide to the president, I had been under the microscope ever since entering the White House orbit. Every day I came into work, I was auditioning for the job. Scowcroft, Gulley—everyone in the Military Office from the drivers on up—were watching how I comported myself in the context of power and the powerful personalities who wielded it. If any one of them had doubts about me, I would most likely have been asked politely but firmly to vacate the premises.

With the exception of one person—ironically, the president himself—you can't work in the White House without being thoroughly vetted. I later learned that while I was being scrutinized, my background was being investigated as well. FBI agents visited my high school teachers, interviewed former employers, and dug into my family background, as well as that of my wife. (Her parents were both from Sweden, a fact that had apparently required deeper digging: they couldn't have any Swedish spies hanging around in the White House.)

From San Clemente to Pennsylvania Avenue to this night on the *Sequoia*, I was learning to parse my behavior: be amicable without being overfriendly, deferential without being obsequious, reserved without being aloof. On the yacht, my mentor and guide was Jack Brennan. I couldn't have asked for a better man to show me the way.

I'd known Jack since the midsixties, when he was my gunnery instructor at Fort Sill, Oklahoma. He has two qualities I admire equally: a sense of honor (he earned a Purple Heart in Vietnam) and a sense of humor. Jack also has a quality that I believe is crucial to being a military aide to the president: the ability to take a situation seriously without taking *himself* seriously.

For most of the two-hour boat ride, Jack had been in good spirits. He gave me a tour and showed me the ropes, always maintaining a discreet distance from the president. Careful not to intrude on the man's privacy, he stayed close enough to make himself available if he was needed. As the evening drew to a close, darkness enveloping the river and the yacht, Nixon withdrew to the salon belowdecks, while Rebozo, more of a social animal, stayed behind to chat with the crew.

Following Nixon's exit, I detected a slight shift in Jack's mood—as if his good spirits had withdrawn with the president. It was another one of those ropes I had to learn. A military aide will see the president, and potentially come to know him, as no one else will. The aide has to be able to anticipate the president's needs—whether it's for a pipe or an aircraft carrier—but as much as he may come to understand and feel for the man, he has to keep his own feelings in check. He has to maintain that middle distance, not only physically, but emotionally as well.

I'm sure Jack sensed, far better than I did, the profound import of that moment—Nixon alone with his thoughts, reflecting on the choice he had likely made that evening at dinner. Belowdecks, the president sat at Truman's piano. He was playing "God Bless America."

Wake-up Call

So now another ghost wandered the halls of the White House—the living, breathing specter of President Richard M. Nixon. It was simply a matter of time before the elephant left the room. Until then, however: the show must go on.

Eight o'clock in the morning, Saturday, August 3, the phone with the White House icon on it rang in my quarters at Bolling Air Force Base. I pounced on it.

"Major Barrett."

"Yes!"

"Sir, you're supposed to be at Camp David. Mr. Gulley has sent a car for you."

Shit. This was news to me. Could I be fired for something I didn't know? Could I be fired from a job I didn't even have? In a Bill Gulley heartbeat. *I didn't get the memo* wasn't going to cut it.

Thankfully, it didn't have to. When I arrived at the barracks in Camp David—the president's country retreat in Maryland—I was ready to get reamed. But instead I was let off the hook. The White House may have the most sophisticated communications system on Earth, but what the hell good is it if people don't *talk*? It was just another snafu (army speak for *situation normal: all fucked up*).

I reported to the dining room at Aspen Lodge—the president's cabin. I was scheduled for a late breakfast with Nixon's personal secretary, Rose Mary Woods.

My grand tour of presidential environments continued, and this place, Camp David, struck me as the ultimate perk of the office, certainly worthy of FDR's original name for it—Shangri-La. By the nature of the job, presidents never get away from it all, because wherever they go, everything follows. But Camp David, a thirty-minute helicopter jump from the White House, is about as close to a get-out-of-jail-free card as they're going to find.

My brunch with Mrs. Woods was, like the woman herself, polite, pleasant, and unremarkable. But on another level, it was just one more step down the rabbit hole. Rose Mary Woods had been Nixon's gatekeeper from his early days in Congress and, if not for her fierce loyalty to the man—and an eighteen-and-a-half-minute gap in those Oval Office tapes that were gutting his presidency—her name would at some point have slipped into obscurity. Instead, it landed on the cover of *Time* magazine. She claimed that it had been an accident, that she had inadvertently erased the tape; the more likely scenario, given the Nixon White House's propensity for cover-up, was that someone had deliberately deleted an offending section of the recording, and that Woods had thrown herself under the bus. Either way, she was an innocent—collateral damage of the Watergate mess.

Now, here we were breaking bread, me making small talk and she gauging my fitness to work alongside her as army aide to the president. It was all part of the show. Because as we sat there exchanging pleasantries over orange juice and poached eggs, I knew that she knew that I knew that in all likelihood the president would not be president much longer, and he would be in no position to offer me any position at all. We put on quite a performance. We had to. There was no other way to play it. We both had our roles, and we stuck to the script. Everybody in the White House did. You stop the music, and the whole production falls apart. So we all went down the rabbit hole together.

Moving Day

Nixon landed at Camp David that afternoon and spent the next twenty-four hours huddling with his family. The place was no Shangri-La that weekend. There was no letup, as the prognosis over the next few days went from bad to worse to malignant. The biggest mistake Rose Mary Woods made was not erasing enough of the tapes: the most damning witness against the president was the president himself. Support for him in Congress was bottoming out—and the ground was shifting beneath him.

It was around the same time as the yacht ride that conservative Republican senator Barry Goldwater came to the White House to encourage Nixon to resign, as did Tip O'Neill, the Democratic Speaker of the House. Both men explained to him that he did not have the support of either chamber to remain in the Oval Office. Even so, while I didn't hear it directly, I believe it was the conversation with Rebozo on the yacht that convinced Nixon resignation was his best option.

At 5:29 in the morning, July 16, 1945, in the desert sands of south-central New Mexico, the first man-made nuclear device in history was detonated. Prior to the test several of the observers set up a betting pool on the results. Some wagered that the device would be a complete dud, while others bet on degrees of success—measured in kilotons of TNT the explosion would generate. Enrico Fermi, one of the greatest physicists of the twentieth century, offered to take wagers on the possibility of a chain reaction—whether if the atmosphere ignited it would destroy just New Mexico or incinerate the entire world. Here they were, the smartest guys on the planet, and they didn't have a fucking clue.

A similar atmosphere prevailed at the White House that week. We wouldn't know the damage done until after the bomb went off. History wasn't any help because there was no history to go by.

Now there is. In the end, the implosion was contained.

On the evening of August 8, 1974 President Nixon announced to the nation—and world—his retirement from the office, effective the next day. The morning of August 9 was misty, hot, and humid—another typical summer day in DC. Around 9:00 A.M. I made my way from the military aide offices to the East Room. Glancing into offices along the way, I saw desks being cleared, boxes being packed, and documents being shredded.

It was moving day.

Becoming more and more adept at the art of being invisible, I chose a spot off to the side of the East Room and took the scene in. The president, his family standing behind him, spoke to the men and women who had worked for him. His speech the night before had been a painful thing to watch: the television lights highlighting the perspiration on his brow as he visibly trembled from some combination of sorrow, shame, guilt, self-loathing, anger, and exhaustion. But the burden of that day fell most heavily not on Nixon himself, but on his wife, the first lady. Pat Nixon, steadfast and always smiling—except for now, her face a brittle mask—stood behind her husband. But the future must have appeared bleak to her, bound to this man descending into personal depression and professional decline—as though she were tied to the mast of a sinking ship. More collateral damage. Yet, she still carried herself with elegance and grace.

As powerful as presidents are, to my mind—and I think history bears this out—the most amazing person in the White House at any given moment is the first lady. Eleanor Roosevelt, Jacqueline Kennedy, Lady Bird Johnson, Pat Nixon, Betty Ford, and on and on—they've all left an indelible mark on the place.

There was applause, then silence, interrupted by suppressed coughs and the scraping of chairs. Eyes around the room were bloodshot from too little sleep and too much crying. And in his last act as president, he said goodbye—or, in his words, au revoir.

Pat Nixon was a victim of so many things. She didn't have the emotional stamina and heart that Betty Ford had, the ability to withstand what came with being married to the president of the United States, much less one who put himself in such a compromised position as Nixon did. I always felt bad for Pat Nixon.

For myself, I didn't know what to feel or how to act. I was nothing at the White House yet. Here I was, still in the interview stage, but I was given close access to everything that was happening with the changing of the guard. Even so, influenced by everyone around me, I too sensed how sad a day this was. There was a weightiness, a feeling of heaviness over the entire place. You could see in everyone's eyes how devastating this was.

At 10:30 A.M., Nixon climbed the steps of a helicopter waiting on the South Lawn, turned, and made his final wave, giving the V for victory sign in the moment of his complete and utter defeat. On board was his marine aide Jack Brennan, who would retire from the Marine Corps to assume the position of Nixon's civilian chief of staff—a harbinger of things to come for me. Jack Brennan defined loyalty.

At 11:35 A.M., August 9, Nixon handed his letter of resignation to Secretary of State Henry Kissinger. I don't know this to be true, but I have always suspected that Kissinger actually wrote it for Nixon. Somewhere over the country's heartland, Air Force One ceased to be Air Force One, President Nixon became citizen Nixon, and the first lady became simply his wife.

Chicken Little was wrong: the sky wasn't falling. It was just a little rain. No dominos had fallen; there had been no chain reaction. The government was still standing.

The end came. And as with all endings, it was also a beginning.

An Uncertain Beginning

The old crowd had drifted out of the East Room; two hours later a new crowd filed in, giving a standing ovation to the new first family.

Over the coming weeks, almost everyone who had served with Nixon had to go. The dry cleaner was not going to be able to get the Nixon stain out of anyone associated with his administration. It was probably unfair that a number of them were grouped with the Haldeman/Erlichman modus operandi. If you weren't linked to it in an obvious way, it's unlikely you knew what was going on.

The people who did remain from Nixon's presidency into President Ford's mainly existed in parallel universes. There were run-ins and gossip about the two groups vying for the president's ear. The truth is that President Ford's newcomers didn't know many of the finer details typically shared during a transition of power from one president to the next. Those transitions typically occur over a two-month period. That two months' worth of education didn't take place because of the hastiness of Nixon's exit and Ford's ascension.

There were people immune to any contentiousness between the two groups. First—the Secret Service. From everything I experienced, this group lives up to their motto, "You elect 'em, we'll protect 'em." There was no political bias or favoritism—simply blind allegiance to whomever holds the office. I observed the same thing with the White House staff. One president hates runny eggs—the staff produces no runny eggs. The next president prefers runny eggs—that's what the staff provides. It was beautiful to see them turn on a dime.

From my limited time present during Nixon's presidency, he seemed much more guarded and with stricter access than President Ford. Ford had multiple people through whom others could get to him and was quite comfortable with that. He appreciated input from multiple sources, as long as you stayed within proper channels to offer that input. With the proper liaison (and that was whoever served as your boss), you could get to the Oval Office. Just don't circumvent the order of command.

Two very important men who did continue under the new president were Henry Kissinger as secretary of state and his right-hand man, General Brent Scowcroft, who was named national security advisor. Scowcroft was one of the greatest public servants I ever met. He understood the role of a military man in service to the president, his commander in chief. Simply being around Scowcroft, observing how he handled himself, made me better at my job.

Kissinger, the suave, sophisticated Jewish intellectual, was quite a contrast with the plodding, blond-haired Michigander who had unexpectedly been elevated to being leader of the free world. What I came to understand later was how much these two men loved each other.

On one of the occasions when the president had an important decision to make, Kissinger and Scowcroft disagreed on the proper plan of action.

"Well, Brent, I'm sorry," the president said. "But you have to understand. Henry's a lot smarter than me, and I feel like I have to follow his advice."

In over two hundred years, has there ever been another president who said anyone else was smarter than them? It doesn't happen. Unless it's Jerry Ford.

My fellow Americans, our long national nightmare is over. Our constitution works. Our great republic is a government of laws and not of men. Here, the people rule.

And so began the term of the accidental president, Gerald R. Ford. He declared that the "nightmare" was over, but there was still some tossing and turning to do. But now, at least the people putting together the puzzle knew what pieces they had and what pieces they were missing.

Two days after Ford was sworn in, Sunday, I was assigned to go out to his home in Alexandria and accompany the president and his family to morning mass at Immanuel Church on the Hill, near where he lived. I found the president and his wife, Betty, assessing a house in transition, walking among the boxes and the possessions accumulated during their years there. Take this, leave that, purging and reminiscing just as any husband and wife do when leaving one place for another. More moving. I walked a discreet distance behind.

The president came upon several of his old navy uniforms hanging in a closet. He thought for a moment. He hadn't seen them in years. They just took up space. Being the practical man that he was, he made his decision: "I guess we'll have to pack these up and send them to Goodwill."

I suspect it was not the first, and I know it was not the last time that Betty countermanded her husband's orders. She told him he couldn't do that. The matter was out of his hands. What he didn't realize—and Betty did—was that the uniforms didn't belong to him anymore. They belonged to history.

Anyone who has ever packed up their belongings—wrapped the glassware in newspapers, stripped the pictures off the wall, and tossed the kids' clothes in a bag—and prepared for a move knows how stressful it can be. Considering where they were going, the Fords were very much at ease about the whole thing—they might as well have been moving to the house next door. It was a sign of their strength, the support they gave each other. But they weren't the only ones on the move that day.

A little over a hundred miles to the north, my wife Bev was stuffing our lives away in boxes she'd collected from liquor and grocery stores. The difference was, she had to do the purging and reminiscing alone. And, looking back, I wonder—as I focused on the changes taking place in my life as opposed to *our* lives—if the only thing my wife and I had that belonged to history was a happy marriage.

Four days later, the morning of August 15, the sixth day of Ford's presidency, my future arrived. It was waiting for me in the Oval Office, as was the president and a second man I'd never seen before. Bill Gulley had called and said, "Put on your uniform and go over to the Oval Office. The president wants to see you."

When I walked in, I did the only thing I knew to do.

"Sir, Major Barrett reporting for duty."

The president popped up from his chair and came out from behind his desk to meet me halfway. He reached out to give me a vigorous handshake. For a split second I froze: salute or handshake? I couldn't do both—I only had one right hand, and my instinct in this situation was to salute. Finally, and awkwardly, I took the president's hand.

"I'm sorry for the confusion, Major Barrett," he said. "I hope you'll stay with us."

As low-key as ever, this second man introduced himself. What I didn't know at the time—and I doubt few did—was that the quiet man with the modest demeanor would be a prime mover in the Republican Party, and American governance, for the next forty years. Richard (Dick) Cheney had been brought in to the White House to help in the transition from one president to another—to bring order to the chaos. Cheney had the steely discipline to say nothing if he couldn't tell the truth. That drove the press crazy throughout his time on the American political scene.

That was the transition in a nutshell—from the indecency of the previous administration to the fundamental decency of this man. The president apologizing to me? For what? For not becoming president a few weeks earlier? For that awkward moment when I was caught between a salute and a handshake? No, he was apologizing because he thought it the proper and gracious thing to do—sorry for the mess, now let's move forward—and I had only one way to answer it.

"Yes, sir."

I was home.

2

The Mercy Rule

Thinking on Your Feet

Nobody had ever taken such a step before—it was unprecedented, almost unimaginable. The idea of it had been in the works for years, but before the actual day of reckoning, there would be months of planning, intensive research, endless rehearsals, and top-secret reconnaissance, much of it illegal. And once the step was taken, there would be no going back.

At 7:00 A.M., Wednesday, August 7, 1974, two days before Nixon resigned and Ford assumed the presidency, Philippe Petit, a twenty-five-year-old French high-wire artist, stepped out onto a taut steel cable strung between the two towers of the World Trade Center in lower Manhattan. The two towers swayed in the wind, as did the wire. Nonetheless, for forty-five minutes, Petit walked, laughed, danced, and pranced a quarter mile up in the thin air. And just as the sun burned through the morning mist, for a few moments—in a time of political upheaval, economic crisis, and American anxiety—onlookers on the streets below, and on television later, cheered the artist on. He lifted their spirits and showed them what was possible—this man who had become one with the sky.

Twenty-seven years later, on September 11, 2001, the buildings that Petit had made his canvas ceased to exist, wiped away, along with thousands of lives, by terrorists. We are all walking on a wire.

From the country's inception, America's enemies have always stood at the gates, looking for weakness and vulnerabilities. In 1814, the British burned down the White House. In 1941, the Japanese decimated the US Navy fleet in Pearl Harbor. And on 9/11/2001, Al Qaeda militants burned a hole in our heart.

In the summer of 1974, the new President Ford would have to perform his own act of daring. The difference between the president and Philippe Petit was that Ford didn't have the luxury of time. No planning, no rehearsal, no reconnaissance, just a man from Michigan on a high wire.

Armageddon in a Bag

The morning of Thursday, August 16, eight days after Petit tiptoed across the New York skyline, I emerged from the Oval Office walking on air, officially appointed army aide to the president. One of my primary duties: carrying the "football."

In 1962, during the Cuban Missile Crisis, the United States and the Soviet Union contemplated unleashing hell on Earth. The Strategic Air Command, a component of the US military's strategic nuclear strike forces, was ordered to defense readiness condition (DEFCON) 2, described as the "next step to nuclear war." But although the pistol was pulled from the holster, aim taken, and pressure applied, the trigger was never pulled. In the aftermath of the crisis, having stared out into the abyss, President John F. Kennedy had a laundry list of questions and concerns.

If he were away from the White House, with its Situation Room and the red button on his desk that connected him to the Pentagon, how, in the event of imminent nuclear attack, Kennedy wanted to know, was he supposed to communicate with the Joint Chiefs of Staff? And if he should happen to get through to the War Room, to whom would he be speaking and how would they confirm his identity? And last, but certainly not least, he was appalled by the doctrine of mutually assured destruction (MAD)—the theory that both the United States and the Soviet Union would be deterred from launching a nuclear attack by the knowledge that it would lead to retaliation and the annihilation of both sides. In other words, the president's only choice in the event of attack was all-out nuclear war. Kennedy wanted more options.

The upshot: the introduction of the president's emergency satchel, a black leather Zero Halliburton briefcase, weighing in at about thirty pounds and packed full of the stuff that represents the supreme power of the presidency in its most lethal form.

Brent Scowcroft—deputy assistant to the president for national security affairs—initiated me into the satchel's deep, dark secrets. He introduced me to the Black Book, a nine-by-twelve-inch loose-leaf binder containing some seventy-five pages, detailing the president's options in the event of imminent nuclear attack—retaliatory responses printed in red. It presented him with a kind of Chinese menu divided among four primary potential targets: Soviet nuclear forces, Soviet conventional forces, military and political leadership, and finally economic and industrial centers. Each of those main options was broken down into various measured subsets: Major Attack Options, Selected Attack Options, and Limited Attack Options. It seemed to me a lot to put on a man's plate in the face of decimation, but then I didn't have a say in the matter—and didn't want one. I was just the bagman.

Also in the case: a second, thinner black book listing various top-secret American sites—bunkers and airborne command centers—that were at the president's disposal during an emergency; a secure SATCOM (satellite communication) radio and handset enabling him to contact the Joint Chiefs of the military as well as foreign leaders; and a three-by-five-inch card revealing the Gold Codes—revised daily by the National Security Agency—which were the final piece of the puzzle, the launch codes that would send the nuclear missiles screaming across the sky toward their targets.

One of the original options in the president's nuclear playbook had been code-named *Dropkick*. In order to execute a dropkick, one needed a football. Thus christened, the football was handed off to me in August 1974—and, as with his American Express card, the president never left home without it.

Disarming

A confession: being the bearer of such great power in proximity to the man who might potentially wield it was both intriguing and beguiling. I was awestruck, wonderfully overwhelmed—similar, I imagine, to how it must feel to carry a king's scepter or the crown jewels. But it wasn't long before it became routine, a part of the job. I was just another man with a briefcase.

I can't say how many times I've been asked how it felt to have the responsibility that came with the briefcase. I always answered: *Good! If an attack came,* I'd say, *I'd cut the casualties in half. I never could remember the combination of the damned thing.*

Carrying the football, I could rarely let President Ford out of my sight. It wasn't my job to document, protect, or minister to him. He had other people, much better qualified than I, to undertake those critical tasks. My job was simply to be there. I was a delivery device, a button to be pressed if nuclear push came to nuclear shove. When he was on the move, I was on the move, always in *the bubble*—the wandering perimeter, secured by Secret Service agents, enfolding the POTUS like the walls of an amoeba around its nucleus.

Whether he was going down the block or halfway around the world, getting onto an elevator or boarding Air Force One, I (or one of his two other military aides) was right there behind him, sticking to the man like white on rice. I carried the potential for nuclear annihilation into church on Sunday mornings, onto a golf cart Sunday afternoons, and into the halls of the Capitol any day of the week.

There was one exception to the white-on-rice rule. When traveling with the president, once he was secured in a hotel room, I would hand the football off to the White House Communications Agency team. WHCA (pronounced *walk-ah*) is an elite military unit whose mission is to ensure that the president and his staff "can communicate anywhere, anytime, by any means to anyone in the world."

The White House contains the most sophisticated state-of-the-art communications infrastructure in the world. It's WHCA's job to see to it that that vast, intricate, all-encompassing network is already in place before the president arrives at his next stop. By the time the president arrives at his hotel, a room very close to his has been hooked into a web of telecommunications and satellites that most of us don't even know exist. And it is in that room that the football sits while the president sleeps at night.

I'd like to tell you what's in that room, but if I did I'd have to kill you. No, that's not really true. The reason I can't tell you what's in a WHCA-enhanced hotel room is that I was never invited into one. For a communications agency, WHCA doesn't communicate much. To anyone other than those who have a "need to know"—and I did not—WHCA is the blackest of black holes.

When I would board Air Force One, I would place the football at the feet of the communicator, the head of the WHCA team on that trip, as I boarded the plane. On a trip to France, the location of the French president's greeting of President Ford was changed just as we landed, from one place to another, by a couple hundred feet. I was walking with my French counterpart, their president's military aide, to the new location for the presidential greeting. Suddenly I realized I had forgotten to get the football from the communicator before disembarking. All I could think about was which smart-ass press person was going to ask me where the football was.

We got in the cars for the motorcade trip to where the presidents would be meeting—a line of at least twenty vehicles. I was in what's called the control car—the third vehicle in line, behind the president's limo and the Secret Service's SUV. The president's chief of staff, at that time Donald Rumsfeld, was in the front seat of the control car, and I was in the back seat with Terry O'Connell, the civilian aide, and Dave Kennerly, the president's photographer. I was trying to figure out what to do, how the hell I was going to get the football back without making any more of a damn fool of myself.

All of a sudden a vehicle came screaming down the road on the left side of all the cars in the motorcade. It pulled up right next to our vehicle. Both vehicles stopped. Herb Oldenburg, an army master sergeant and the man who had been looking after presidential luggage and all of his traveling party's luggage for twenty years, rolled down the window and stuck his head out next to our car.

"Hey, Bob," he said, "do you have everything you want?"

"No," I sheepishly said.

"Come closer."

When we arrived at our destination and I got out of the control car the second time, I had the football.

The press was always asking to see what was in the football. To satisfy them, I had the White House kitchen staff make some salami sandwiches, wrap them in wax paper, and put them in the briefcase that held the football. They gathered around me, excited to finally see what had been verboten for so long. I entered the combination of the lock, slowly opened the case, showed them what was inside, and told them not to ask again. They didn't during my tenure as military aide.

———

Sharing elevators and nuclear-launch codes with the president meant I had the highest possible clearance—the same clearance as the president's chief of staff and the pilot of Air Force One. Didn't matter. WHCA couldn't care less about my clearance. *Need to know*—that was the operative phrase in the White House. If you didn't need to know, then you *didn't need to know*. No one—with the possible exception of Scowcroft—knew everything. Knowledge in the White House was like salami—each of us had a slice of it, but not the whole sausage.

When I was named military aide to the president, it was Bill Gulley who cut my slice, telling me everything I needed to know. His advice was simple and clear: "Don't fuck it up."

Sound, sensible advice for anyone, anywhere, doing just about anything. Including the president of the United States. *Don't fuck it up*. The problem for the new president that August—Ford—was that his predecessor had not heeded that advice. Nixon had screwed things up royally, and now it was left to Ford to unscrew things—a task akin to removing the chocolate from chocolate milk.

Bit by a Dead Bee

Following the 1972 elections, House minority leader Gerald R. Ford seriously considered retiring from politics. After twenty-plus years in Congress, seven as minority leader, it seemed to him that he had gone as far as he could in government, his days of public service over.

He was mistaken. The public, it turned out, had a lot more work for him to do.

As House minority leader, Ford had run an office with a staff of about twenty-five people. Now, in the Oval Office, he presided over more than a million employees working for the executive branch of the federal government, he served as commander in chief to more than two million active-duty military personnel, and he answered to a constituency of more than two hundred million American souls. And each and every one of them, no matter where he (or she) sat—in an office in the West Wing of the White House, at a corner bar in Brooklyn, or at a kitchen table in Kalamazoo—had his (or her) own agenda.

Lower prices. Raise wages. Create more jobs. Find more oil. Use less oil. Protect the environment. Spend more. Spend less. Contain the Soviets, corral the Chinese, keep an eye on the Middle East, and don't forget the Far East. Negotiate. Compromise. Don't give an inch . . .

The welter of issues and conflicts surrounding and hounding the president were never farther from him than the morning papers he loved and the meetings he called. But of all the questions, concerns, and powerful personalities that Ford confronted—by necessity speeding up his on-the-job training—one man and *his* agenda loomed largest, casting a long dark shadow across his fledgling presidency.

In the 1944 movie *To Have and Have Not*, starring Humphrey Bogart and Lauren Bacall, a drunken sailor named Eddie asks everyone he comes across: "Was you ever bit by a dead bee?" To which they all answer *no*. Thirty years later, if the inebriated Eddie had happened to stumble into the Oval Office and ask President Ford the same question, he would have had to say *Yes, I have been bit by a dead bee.*

Nixon may have left the building, his presidency dead, but the stingers he had left behind were coming out of the White House woodwork.

Who owned the warehouse full of papers and some 3,700 hours of tape recordings produced by the Nixon White House? Were they the former president's or were they US government property? Could China and the Soviet Union be trusted? Nixon had opened the door to both of our superpower rivals, but would they now slam the door shut—and start rattling their sabers again—in the face of a new and untested president? And what about Vietnam? Nixon had, in his words, achieved "peace with honor," but the reality on the ground was: there was neither peace nor honor in Southeast Asia.

But the biggest stinger of all was the lingering question of what to do about the man himself. What to do about Nixon.

After he resigned and went back to San Clemente, Ford would occasionally go out to visit the former president. Ford had a deep and abiding loyalty to and respect for America's institutions—the US Senate, the House, the Supreme Court, all the cabinet positions, and the presidency. Ford respected Nixon as a person, but he honored him as a person who had held the office of president of the United States.

Wild Ride

King Hussein of Jordan, whose reign over that Middle Eastern nation lasted from 1952 to his death in 1999, was a small man who lived large—an avid sportsman, motorcycle enthusiast, and race car driver and a pilot of his own jets and helicopters. Hussein was the first foreign head of state to visit the White House during the Ford presidency. Friday, August 16, 11:30 A.M., exactly one week after Nixon's resignation, Hussein met with Ford and Secretary of State Henry Kissinger in the Oval Office—the transitional nature of the place evidenced by the empty bookshelves. Some had suggested that the visit should be postponed and rescheduled, but Ford, recognizing the importance of maintaining the appearance of a smooth, uninterrupted exercise of American governance and power, insisted that it go on as planned.

Before the meeting, Kissinger advised the president not to ride with King Hussein in the helicopter he would be piloting.

As they met, Hussein explained to Ford that "Secretary Kissinger was very kind to be one of my passengers."

To which Kissinger replied, "I became religious very quickly."

King Hussein was a daredevil—not only in his choice of hobbies but also in his choice of policies and geopolitical pursuits. He was an anomaly: an Arab leader who recognized the benefits of achieving peace with Israel.

Risking his popularity and his life (he had been the target of numerous assassination attempts), Hussein met secretly over the years with Israeli diplomats and leaders, determined to find a path to coexistence. Here was a man who ruled an arid, virtually landlocked country in one of the most volatile regions on Earth—surrounded by Israel to the west, the Soviet-backed, saber-rattling countries of Syria and Iraq to the north and east, and Saudi Arabia to the south—and, despite it all, managed to turn Jordan into an oasis of relative peace and prosperity.

Ford must have seen a kindred spirit in the king. A man facing pressure on all sides, powerful forces urging him to follow their lead and to act in their self-interest—all the while keeping his cool, comfortable in his own skin, whether flying loop de loops in his helicopter or guiding the ship of state. Hussein had been at the wheel for a couple of decades, Ford for a couple of days. He would have to learn on the fly.

A visit by a foreign leader sends ripples throughout the White House. What it meant for me, that Friday, was a late night at the office.

As military aide to the president, my job, aside from carrying the football, was simple: make life easier for the commander in chief. A president is often on the move, whether down Pennsylvania Avenue or halfway around the world. Our job as military aides is to make sure he has what he needs, when he needs it, where he needs it. Paper clips, armored limos, helicopters, marching bands, all the assets required for a successful presidential trip—and the C-5 Galaxy cargo planes to haul the stuff into place. As military aides we were constantly in the process of pre-planning or planning for the next trip or mopping up after the last one.

It could be a massive undertaking, but remarkably, for all the moving parts, the machine always ran smoothly. Sure there were occasional screwups along the way, but by and large the military, especially with regard to its responsibilities to the commander in chief, has a low tolerance for idiots. They are sequestered before being able to do any damage to the process.

That Friday night no cargo planes would be required. The work was all in-house. I'd put on my dress uniform, the snazzy short white jacket with the gold braid and epaulets, and attended the first state dinner hosted by this president and first lady. It was a joyous night.

The *New York Times* summed it up: "Any resemblance between this bouncy evening and state dinners of recent years was purely protocol. The menu was standard, there were the usual toasts and trumpets, but everyone, it seemed, was having fun. . . . It was, someone said, like a celebration at the end of a war."

After dinner, the president and Mrs. Ford, King Hussein, and his gorgeous wife, Queen Alia, danced nonstop for over an hour. There was jitterbugging, rock-and-roll, champagne, and laughter. Ding, dong, the wicked witch was dead. The stiff formality, the gloom of the Nixon years, gave way to the joie de vivre of the Fords. They actually enjoyed having a good time, and for one night, at least, the weight of the world was lifted off the city of Washington's shoulders.

Attending state dinners was just one of the perks of my job. Several hours after midnight, I went home to another. Fort Belvoir is a sprawling US Army installation on the banks of the Potomac, about a half-hour drive from the White House. My home was in the Belvoir Village section of the garrison. Nestled in the wooded riverside bluffs, it had been built in the Colonial Revival style in the 1930s—spacious, secluded, and totally disproportionate to my rank. But I worked for the commander in chief and was quartered accordingly. Or, I should say, Bev and the kids were. What with the frequent travel, the late nights, and working weekends, mine was an itinerant life. It suited me.

Proximity to power gives you access to far more than just decent housing. As I would come to discover over the coming months and years, it acts as one hell of an aphrodisiac. And the travel, both here and abroad, provided the opportunity to use it. Temptation was not hard to find, but it was hard to resist. Perks. And pitfalls. Thrills, chills, and spills. Yes, it was going to be a wild ride.

Troubled Waters

On March 8, 1968, the Soviet submarine K-129 mysteriously lost power and sank in the North Pacific. Its entire crew and three nuclear-tipped missiles were lost. The Soviet navy launched a massive search but failed to locate the missing sub. The US Navy, however, armed with superior technology—a chain of underwater listening posts designed to track foreign submarines—pinpointed the wreck 1,500 miles northwest of Hawaii. To the Central Intelligence Agency, this was the mother lode. The trick was salvaging the vessel—with its nuclear-tipped missiles and code room—and hoisting it from the sea floor, three miles below the surface, without arousing Soviet suspicions.

Enter the reclusive billionaire industrialist and longtime friend and asset of the agency, Howard Hughes. The CIA had set into motion the design and construction of the *Glomar Explorer*—a vessel some two football fields long with a massive mechanical claw concealed within its hold. Hughes agreed to act as a cover, putting his name on the project and saying that the ship would be used to mine manganese nodules from the ocean floor.

On June 20, 1974, the *Hughes Glomar Explorer* set sail from Long Beach, California. Less than two months later, days into his presidency, Ford faced one of his first critical tests: deciding the fate of Project Azorian—the CIA code name for the half-billion-dollar project to raise the Soviet submarine from the ocean floor.

The *Glomar Explorer* was on-site, but a Soviet trawler had been spotted nearby, photographing the strange vessel. Ford's national security team—Kissinger, Scowcroft, Defense Secretary James Schlesinger, and CIA director William Colby—briefed him on the tense state of affairs in the North Pacific. If Soviet sailors attempted to board the *Explorer*, its largely civilian crew would be defenseless. The cover story would be blown—and the Kremlin would no doubt blow its top. If Ford ordered

US Navy warships into the area, it would only compel the Soviets to do the same, creating a standoff between the navies of the two superpowers. Another hot mess.

Despite the dangers, Ford ultimately decided that the potential rewards—salvaging the submarine and all its secrets—outweighed the potential risks. He figured he was holding a pretty good hand. For all the Soviets knew, they were taking pictures of a commercial vessel and were unlikely to chance setting off an international incident by boarding her. And they never did.

In the end, the mission failed: the submarine broke apart, most of it falling back to the bottom of the sea, where it remains today. But what the incident does provide is a window into Ford's way of thinking. When a decision had to be made, he'd listen to the experts, weigh his options, make a choice, and move on—never second-guessing himself. There was always another dustup, crisis, or fire to be put out around the corner.

Parallel Universes

As I mentioned earlier, in the early days of the Ford presidency, the White House supported two distinct yet parallel outfits. I liken it to two army divisions, under the same command, marching in the same direction, aware of each other's existence, but both fighting for the same prize: in this case, the president's ear.

On one side, the veteran holdovers from the Nixon administration. On the other, the new blood, Ford's team. The two factions eyed each other warily, sharpening their respective tongues and elbows. For their part, the Nixonites said to themselves: *as soon as we get these Ford people schooled everything will be all right.* The Ford folks, meanwhile, countered: *as soon as we get these Nixon people out of here everything will be all right.* It was a situation ripe for palace intrigue.

In the final days of the Nixon administration, the general—Alexander Haig—had been the man behind the curtain. By controlling access to the reeling president and making decisions in Nixon's name, Haig had in essence been running the White House and, by extension, the country. He deserved credit for keeping the ship of state on course while Nixon, like Captain Queeg in *The Caine Mutiny*, obsessed over who stole his strawberries. But now, with Ford in the Oval Office, Haig's position became problematic.

Privately, Haig believed that, for all Nixon's faults, he was the victim of an insurrection, overthrown by his enemies in the government, the press, and the Establishment—what we now call the *Deep State*. Which brings me to another parallel line I want to draw, this one stretching across forty-plus years.

How does today's political environment—the one ushered in by the 2016 election victory of Donald Trump over Hillary Clinton—stack up against the one I bore witness to during the Ford years? I'm aiming at a moving target. History's not going to stop for my benefit. Life in Washington accelerates at a feverish pace, the political reality changing by the hour, moving at the speed of an early-morning presidential tweet or late-night leak to the press. But as I look back and move forward, simultaneously reflecting on and chasing history, my hope is that by the end of these memoirs, I will have gained enough perspective to draw a line from the past to the present that will point to the future.

Haig was a general in the US Army who served with distinction in a foreign war, Vietnam. A supremely ambitious man, he used his position of command in the military as a stepping-stone to a position of power in government. Replace Vietnam with Afghanistan and Iraq, and you have an exact description of Michael Flynn, appointed by President Trump to be his national security advisor. The primary difference between the two men is that Haig was largely successful, an astute political animal who knew his way around the corridors of power. Flynn, on the other hand, couldn't get out of his own way. Washington ate him up and spit him out, forcing him to resign after just twenty-four days in his office. He's an excellent example of the Peter Principle—a man rising to the level of his own incompetence.

Both Haig and Flynn represent the potential danger of a transition from a position of authority in the military to one in the government. Certainly, there are those who have made the transition successfully—from Dwight Eisenhower to Colin Powell to Brent Scowcroft. But for every General Eisenhower there is a General Douglas MacArthur—great warriors who are great failures in civilian government. As a military man myself, I can give orders. I can take orders. And I know when to shut up. Flynn failed at the third of these precepts. Haig, in the early days of the Ford administration, stumbled over all three.

In all but name, Haig had been acting president under Nixon. Now, under Ford, he determined to maintain the status quo—to control access to the president and thus control the presidency. He had taken the hill, he held the high ground—and he wasn't going to give it back. But now Haig was the one counting his strawberries. Someone else was steering the ship. Haig ran into a buzz saw named Donald Rumsfeld.

Rumsfeld and Ford had been close ever since serving together in Congress during the sixties. A midwesterner and navy vet like the new president, Rumsfeld had been instrumental in Ford's rise to minority leader in the House. And although he had served as counselor to the president under Nixon, by the time Watergate hit the fan, he was far enough away—serving as US ambassador to NATO in Belgium—to avoid the mess. His experience as an administrator, as well as Ford's familiarity with him, made Rumsfeld a natural selection to head up the transition team. And for his part, Rumsfeld was eager to return from the hinterlands of Europe to the center of American power.

His first order of business was to kick-start the process of maneuvering Haig out of the White House. It was the right move. Haig's heavy hand would only hold the new president back. But Rumsfeld did not come without flaws of his own—flaws that just about everyone seemed to recognize except for one man: President Ford. It was one of Ford's weaknesses: giving everyone the benefit of the doubt. Or perhaps it was a strength. He expected the best out of people, and many of us sought to rise to those expectations.

Rumsfeld wore his ambition on his sleeve, his agenda clear. He had the mind of a chess player, always thinking several moves—and years—ahead. The ultimate move he envisioned would be from the chair in front of the president's desk to the one behind it. Aspiring to be president is not an unusual desire in Washington. Politicians are like mountain climbers. Few are content to make it halfway up the Matterhorn. Most want to be king of the hill. The problem with Rumsfeld was, he wanted it too much.

Overall, Rumsfeld served the president well, first as chief of staff and later as secretary of defense. But over the next two years, some of the calculations he made in pursuit of his own ends would prove costly—and there would be casualties.

Who Your Friends Are

No matter what your work environment—whether it's the back of a garbage truck, the jungles of Vietnam, or the halls of the White House—it pays to know who your friends are. Otherwise you're walking on eggshells all day—trying so hard not to screw up, you're bound to do so. In my case, for instance, knowing that Bill Gulley—as tough and gruff as he was—stood behind me gave me the confidence and courage I needed to move forward rather than hang back. That's what a good commander does for his troops.

Gulley was a marine and Brent Scowcroft's assistant. I'll never forget his assessment of what it meant to be president of the United States.

"As president, Bob, he doesn't have much," Gulley said. "Okay, so he lives in a public house [the White House]. But as commander in chief, he has

everything—airplanes, helicopters, boats, protection, investigations—the
list goes on and on and on."

Gulley delivered the military goods in Scowcroft's name—and Scowcroft
trusted him implicitly. Gulley had been assisting the president since Johnson's administration. If the Secret Service asked for something he thought
was frivolous, he had no problem telling them to forget it.

"They're asking for a helicopter over such and such a place," I told
him once.

"Tell the head of the Secret Service to call me and tell me why. If justified, they got it. If not, no way."

As part of my duties, I arranged a small event for the president and had
a small army band to play for it. Gulley, once a marine always a staunch
marine, started yelling every curse word in the book at me.

"Who the fuck booked this piece of shit army unit when the marine
band was available?" he demanded.

I apologized profusely. Bill Gulley was not someone you wanted to cross.

As a soldier, I'd developed an instinct for identifying those I could trust.
It's not about who has the most medals on his chest or the most money in
his pocket. It's about who has the most steel in his spine. Honor. Character.
Loyalty. Whatever word you choose, what it comes down to is: who has
your back? And I knew, in a New York minute, that Dick Cheney had
mine. And, more importantly, he had the president's. Cheney was one of
the good guys.

You'd never know that from the sinister portrait of Cheney that emerged
later in his political life. In the post-9/11 world, as vice president in the
George W. Bush administration, Cheney was painted as some kind of
right-wing, warmongering Attila the Hun. Nothing could be further from
the truth.

Formerly a deputy to Rumsfeld in the Nixon administration, Cheney
was named deputy assistant to President Ford and later succeeded Rumsfeld as chief of staff. He was the yin to Rumsfeld's yang—a man of quiet

efficiency with a subtle sense of humor and no personal agenda, much like Ford himself. Cheney got things done without getting credit for it. One thing I've always believed about Dick: when he can't speak the truth, he has the uncanny ability and discipline to remain quiet. In Washington, a town where everyone loves the sound of his or her own voice, that's a unique talent.

Dick Cheney had every person's back who worked in the White House. He was extremely loyal to the president and to everyone the president surrounded himself with. If someone screwed something up, he never threw them under the bus. He was very much like the president himself—they both were excellent leaders, who always led by example. I developed a deep affection and respect for Dick Cheney because of his devotion and character during Ford's presidency. This was one man who never tried to take advantage of his position.

Ford needed people like Cheney as two monumental questions loomed over his administration:

How to dispose of a piece of the past (Nixon)?

And how to dole out a share of the future (the vice presidency)?

To answer those two questions, he needed to know that those closest to him were looking after the interests of the country and of the presidency rather than trading on their access to the Oval Office to further their own ends. These were some of the key players—Ford's silent partners and foxhole buddies—who would ultimately help to define his presidency:

Bob Hartmann, former newspaperman from Los Angeles and longtime consigliere and speechwriter to Ford ("our long national nightmare is over"). Where Ford gave everyone the benefit of the doubt, Hartmann gave it to no one—the perfect counterweight to the president.

Jack Marsh, a gentle small-town lawyer who was a big-time negotiator. Ford didn't care that he was a Democrat—there was no one he trusted more. Selfless to the point of invisibility, Marsh spoke quietly, behind closed doors, but his words carried enormous weight. Access meant nothing to him. Years later I learned that, though he was one of Ford's closest advisors, he had never once flown on Air Force One. He didn't care about the perks, just that Ford was getting good counsel.

Philip Buchen, Ford's former law partner back in Michigan, who had known him since the 1940s. Prior to Nixon's resignation, Buchen had formed a secret team to prepare for the transition—a career-threatening move that could have been construed as an act of insurrection if the Nixon people had caught on.

Benton Becker, a Justice Department lawyer who had served as Ford's lead counsel in both the House and Senate hearings to confirm him as vice president. He had protected then-congressman Ford from meddling by Alexander Haig and now stood legal guard as special counsel to President Ford.

Melvin Laird, Ford's closest ally in the sixties when they served in Congress. Later, working in the Nixon White House, Laird had prodded Nixon to put forward Ford's name as vice president to replace the disgraced Spiro Agnew, and now he would head the search for a new vice president.

It would take all their political savvy, constitutional dexterity, and sheer guts to navigate the murky waters ahead—and get Ford through the Scylla and Charybdis awaiting him. On one side, deciding Nixon's fate. On the other, handing out the plum of the vice presidency. No matter what course they took, enemies would be made and there'd be blood in the water.

Rocky Road

In 1974, the Oscar for Best Picture went to *The Sting*, a movie about a couple of con men starring Paul Newman and Robert Redford. The Emmy for Outstanding Drama Series on television went to a British drama about money and class, *Upstairs, Downstairs*. And in the one hundredth running of the Kentucky Derby, an American thoroughbred named Cannonade took home the roses. But the real horse race of 1974 took place in Washington, and the greatest prize was in the hands of Gerald R. Ford.

From the moment he ascended from the vice presidency to the presidency, the speculation, handicapping, and jockeying for position had begun: Who would Ford appoint to replace himself as vice president?

Names floated to the surface: Governor William Scranton of Pennsylvania, Senator Howard Baker of Tennessee, former attorney general Elliot Richardson, Senator Mark Hatfield of Oregon, and Senator Barry Goldwater of Arizona among them. Many promptly sank out of sight. They were too liberal, too conservative, too close to Nixon, or too far from the center.

Pressure was applied. Holmes Tuttle, a Los Angeles car dealer and major Republican fundraiser, put a call in to Ford, suggesting that the governor of California, former movie star Ronald Reagan, would be well cast. Reagan didn't land the role—not yet anyway—and over the next several years he'd prove to be a burr under Ford's saddle.

As great a prize as the vice presidency was, the search for the right person to fill it posed just as great a dilemma to Ford. He had three requirements for the potential nominee: the individual would have to be someone of national stature, who could be approved by a Congress dominated by the opposition party, and who could deliver electoral votes to the Ford-led ticket in his 1976 presidential reelection bid.

By the beginning of Ford's second week in the office, the list had been narrowed down to two names: George Herbert Walker Bush and Nelson Rockefeller.

Bush had solid credentials as a war hero and party loyalist. A member of what we have come to call "the Greatest Generation," he served with distinction as a naval aviator in the South Pacific during World War II, completing a bombing run even as his aircraft caught fire. The son of a former Republican senator from Connecticut, Prescott Bush, George graduated from Yale and moved to West Texas to make his fortune in oil. Following his father into politics, he became the first Republican to represent Houston in the House and later served as the US ambassador to the United Nations. In 1973 Nixon named him chairman of the Republican National Committee.

The western wing of the party—those who had supported either Goldwater or Reagan for the vice presidency—now threw their weight behind Bush. He was young, conservative, and an adopted son of the West; he had supported Goldwater in his 1964 run for the presidency; and, most importantly, he was *not* Nelson Rockefeller.

Although Goldwater lost the 1964 presidential election by a historic margin, his nomination to lead the Republican ticket that year was a harbinger of things to come. The Grand Old Party was slowly but surely moving south and west (which makes the election in 2016 of Republican New York businessman Donald Trump all the more remarkable). Rockefeller represented everything that many of the growing base of southern and western Republicans detested—a leader of the Eastern establishment, perceived as an elitist, a moderate at best, a progressive at worst.

A member of one of the wealthiest families in America, Nelson Rockefeller was the grandson of John D. Rockefeller, founder of Standard Oil—the progenitor of today's Exxon and Mobil. Nelson took an early interest in public service and politics, serving in various capacities in the Franklin Roosevelt, Truman, and Eisenhower administrations. In 1958, he was elected governor of New York and won reelection to the office for three more terms. His success in New York was not matched nationally, as his three bids for the Republican nomination for president, in 1960, 1964, and 1968, all came up short.

I always liked Rocky. As my governor in the late fifties and sixties, he struck me as someone who genuinely cared about his constituents. Almost a regular guy—a regular guy worth close to a billion dollars. And very intelligent—the man was a thousand solutions in search of a problem. One of the reasons Rockefeller failed to win the Republican nomination was his infidelity and divorce (in another glaring contrast with Trump). He deserved better on the national stage—and now it was up to Ford to decide whether to put him one heartbeat away from the office he had long coveted but never secured.

Now that it was down to two, the real sniping began. Bush and Rockefeller would have to run the gauntlet, dodging blows, many of the shots coming from inside the White House, "unnamed sources" leaking negative stories to the media. One story tied Bush to a Nixon slush fund. A second reported that Rockefeller's money had been used to disrupt the 1972 Democratic Convention. If you wanted to tar someone in those days, all you had to do was mention him in the same sentence as Nixon and his dirty tricks.

Friday, August 16, one week into Ford's presidency, the *New York Times* reported: "some see a bad sign for Rockefeller and Bush in Ford's long study." Whether the stories were true or not, it was clear that the ghosts of Nixon and Watergate were holding the country hostage and holding Ford back. And now, those unnamed sources had leaked a third name to reporters, a compromise candidate for the vice presidency: Donald Rumsfeld.

A Little Confused

Ford and his advisors recognized that the longer the process went on, the messier it would get. He would have to make his choice that weekend and make his announcement early the next week. But first, a diversion—a welcome escape from the sharp claws and noxious clamor of Washington.

A little before 9:00 A.M., Monday, August 19, Air Force One took off from Andrews Air Force Base—Ford taking his first out-of-town trip as president. He was headed to one of his favorite cities, his kind of town, Chicago, to address the annual national convention of the Veterans of Foreign Wars (VFW). Assigned to accompany the president, I could see he was in a fine mood, talking amiably with several of the congressmen and the pool of reporters on board. But as the plane made its approach to O'Hare International Airport in Chicago, his mood turned.

Five days before, on August 14, in the eastern Mediterranean, the
Turkish military had launched an invasion of Cyprus, dividing the island
nation in two and forcibly removing more than a third of the country's
Greek population from their homes. The Greek Cypriots, blaming America
for not stepping in to stop the Turkish invasion, called for a protest this
Monday the 19th at the American embassy in the outskirts of Nicosia,
the capital of Cyprus. Around noon, 5:00 A.M. in Washington, some four
hundred demonstrators appeared at the compound, the protest quickly
turning violent. They threw stones, then doused embassy cars with gasoline
and set them on fire. Then there were gunshots.

As I later discovered, Henry Kissinger had called Ford on Air Force
One to tell him that the recently named US ambassador to Cyprus,
Rodger Davies, and a young woman aide had both been shot dead. As the
president prepared to address the VFW, the killing was a grim reminder
of the cost of war and of the need for the United States to extricate itself
from past entanglements—Vietnam and Watergate—and confront the
critical issues and events unfolding at home and abroad.

As if to underscore the predicament that Ford—and the country—faced,
as he and his wife climbed down the stairs of Air Force One to greet
the assorted local dignitaries gathered on the tarmac, the public address
announcer stepped up to the microphone and welcomed "the president and
Mrs. Nixon!" Ever the gentleman, and recognizing the man's embarrassment, Ford smiled and shook his head.

"Don't worry," I heard him say. "We're all a little confused."

Broad Shoulders

The VFW convention was held at the Conrad Hilton Hotel in downtown
Chicago—the site six years earlier of a violent confrontation, during the
1968 Democratic National Convention, between the city's police force and

Vietnam war protestors. Some 10,000 demonstrators were met by over 20,000 police and National Guardsmen in what was later called a "police riot." The bloody clash in the surrounding streets, which had been broadcast nationally, was a harsh reflection of the deep divisions in American society. The echoes of that clash still reverberated across the country and could be heard in President Ford's speech to the VFW that night.

At most events, as military aide to the president, I would be kept in the background. But for this crowd, many of them in uniform, with medals and ribbons hanging proudly from their hats and chests, I was placed at the base of the stage, facing the thousands of veterans and their spouses. They greeted the president—the commander in chief—with thunderous applause. He was, after all, a decorated veteran of the Second World War. As Ford spoke, however, the warm reception quickly cooled.

In my first words as president of all the people, I acknowledged a power higher than the people, Who commands not only righteousness but love, not only justice but mercy.

Unlike my last two predecessors, I did not enter this office facing the terrible decisions of a foreign war. But, like President Truman and President Lincoln before him, I found on my desk, where the buck stops, the urgent problem of how to bind up the nation's wounds. And I intend to do that. . . .

Accordingly, in my first week at the White House office, I directed the Attorney General of the United States and the Secretary of Defense to report personally to me, before September 1, on the status of some 50,000 of our countrymen convicted, charged, under investigation or still sought for violations of the Selective Service Act or the Uniform Code of Military Justice—offenses loosely described as desertion and draft dodging. . . .

All, in a sense, are casualties; still abroad or absent without leave from the real America. I want them to come home, if they want to work their way back. . . .

All wars are the glory and agony of the young. In my judgment, these young Americans should have a second chance to contribute their fair share to the rebuilding of peace among ourselves and with all nations.

I am throwing the weight of my presidency into the scales of justice on the side of leniency. . . .

You could have heard a pin—or Purple Heart—drop. President Ford had deliberately chosen the toughest crowd in America to deliver this message of renewal and salvation. He knew, in these early days of his presidency, that he had to make clear his strength, individualism, and willingness to break from the past. He had come to the City of Broad Shoulders to demonstrate that he had some broad shoulders of his own.

The next day, Tuesday, August 20, back in the White House, the president took one more step in the healing process. That morning I found myself in the office of the personal secretaries to the president—in essence, a waiting room to the Oval Office. I don't recall what mission brought me to the room, but I do remember who I found there, waiting to see Ford: Governor Nelson Rockefeller.

"How are you?" he asked, leaning forward as if we had met before. I said fine, thank you, and added that I had been born in Brooklyn and raised on Long Island. Now he was smiling, shaking my hand, clapping me on the shoulder like we were old buddies from the neighborhood.

"Goddammit," he boomed, "a New Yorker! We got to stick together."

The man's personality filled the room—and now it would take up residence in the Ford administration.

The president had made his choice and late that day would announce the nomination of Rockefeller for vice president. The Rumsfeld balloon had popped soon after it was floated. He fulfilled none of the three requirements. Rumsfeld lacked national stature, there was no guarantee that his nomination would breeze through congressional hearings, and he could not be counted on to deliver a single electoral vote in 1976. The stories tying Bush and Rockefeller to Nixonian dirty tricks were brushed aside by Ford and his advisors as shadowy allegations from shadowy sources with little or no basis in fact—what some today might call *fake news.*

Naming Bush would have shored up the Republicans, but Ford had to think bigger, beyond the party. Who would shore up America's standing around the world? Rockefeller. He might be the last of a dying breed, but with his credentials and connections abroad, his nomination put an exclamation point on the country's strength and resolve. That Rockefeller might deliver a windfall of electoral votes—New York and Florida—in 1976 was icing on the cake.

The president didn't worry, as some on his staff did—including Rumsfeld—that Ford's star would dim in contrast to a big, bright light like Rockefeller. His only concern was clearing a path to the future, and several roadblocks still stood in the way.

There Is No Answer

An earthquake brings a building down on top of you. If you're lucky enough to survive, you don't ask: What now, what's the best way out of here? Because there is no answer. You react. You scramble. You scratch and claw, pushing things out of the way. You see a ray of light and you scramble some more, following the light until you find your way to the surface. In the summer of 1974, the White House had fallen on top of President Ford, burying him—and, by extension, the entire government and society—in doubt and uncertainty.

We had survived the earthquake—Nixon's fall and resignation—now came the aftershocks. What to do about the former president? Did the country need to purge itself of him through a public trial, or was it better to let it go and move on? That was the question—but there was no *one* answer. In a true democracy, there never is. If there were, there'd be no need for elections.

In a dictatorship, the dictator *is* the answer. In an empire, the emperor *is* the answer. Even if he has no clothes on. In either case, the answer would have been simple: *off with his head*. Nothing in our society is that simple.

The beauty of the American constitution is that it recognizes that, over time and in different circumstances, societies, cultures, and governments evolve. The founding fathers owned slaves and believed women should not have the right to vote. Times change. And so do answers.

As for what to do about Nixon, there might not be one answer, but there was no shortage of opinions.

To the Editor:

Unless Watergate's ultimate lesson is to be that all men are not equal before the law, Mr. Nixon, like any other citizen, must face criminal prosecution for criminal acts. —R.W., New York, N.Y.

An appalling but not amazing aftermath to the [Watergate] saga is the extent to which politicians and public alike are demanding vengeance. —P.H., Roselle, N.J.

There is simply no morally nor legally acceptable alternative to vigorous prosecution of Mr. Nixon, unpalatable as it may be. Any other course would be a clear dereliction of duty. —R.W., Westport, Conn.

Indicting and prosecuting Mr. Nixon would fulfill no legitimate purpose. Mr. Nixon now knows, if he did not before, that no man is above the law. —J.S., New York, N.Y.

If Nixon is allowed to rest on his laurels, such as they are, the whole world will realize that America has one law for the rich and another for the poor, and that the rule of justice here is a mockery. —L.F., Bedford, N.Y.

Those who remain unsatisfied and want Mr. Nixon punished further are not motivated by any desire for justice. It is just malice, pure and simple. —M.B., Jamaica, N.Y.

President Ford was an avid reader of newspapers, devouring five or six by the time he sat down to his English muffin in the morning. The opinion pages and letters to the editor came at the issue from all sides, giving him the view from New York to Grand Rapids, from Wall Street to Main Street. His advisors briefed him on the political consequences. Old friends from the Hill shared their perspectives. Even I put my two cents in. As the president's military aide, I would never volunteer my opinion. But when he asked, I gave it:

We're all Watergate junkies. Some of us are mainlining, some are sniffing, some are lacing it with something else, but all of us are addicted. This will go on and on unless someone steps in and says that we, as a nation, must go cold turkey. Otherwise, we'll die of an overdose.

Snake Canyon

On Sunday, September 8, near Twin Falls, Idaho, stuntman Evel Knievel attempted to fly 1,600 feet across the Snake River Canyon in his steam-powered Skycycle X-2. The attempt failed. A parachute deployed prematurely, and the rocket plummeted to the banks of the Snake River. Knievel suffered minor cuts and scrapes. Halfway around the world, a TWA flight bound from Tel Aviv, Israel, to New York City plunged into the Ionian Sea near Greece, killing all seventy-nine aboard. It was later determined to be the first known instance of an Arab terrorist on a suicide mission bringing down an American aircraft. But the dominating headline in the next day's papers was President Ford's pardon of Richard Milhouse Nixon.

As Ford had said in his speech to the VFW, the buck stopped at his desk. He read all the papers. He listened to all his advisors. He heard what America and the world were saying. But, finally, the burden of the decision rested on his shoulders and his alone. Contemplating that months, maybe years, would pass before the former president could get a fair trial, Ford concluded that "during this long period of delay and potential litigation, ugly passions would again be aroused, our people would again be polarized in their opinions, and the credibility of our free institutions of government would again be challenged at home and abroad. . . . My conscience tells me clearly and certainly that I cannot prolong the bad dreams."

The decision was also a reflection of Gerald Ford, the man, whose small-town Midwestern upbringing taught him that you never kick a man when he's down. Of all the attorneys who weighed in on the subject, perhaps the last word belongs to a woman disguised as a lawyer: Portia in Shakespeare's *The Merchant of Venice*: "The quality of mercy is not strain'd, it droppeth like the gentle rain from heaven."

In the end, Ford decided that he had no choice. But in signing the pardon that day, he spent the lion's share of his political capital. When Ford pardoned Nixon, he knew he might be signing his own political death certificate. But he was resolute in his decision.

"You cannot put a president in the dock," he said, using the British term for putting someone on trial. He took a great leap of faith in the American people—and, unlike Evel Knievel, he would have no parachute in the event of a hard fall.

Burning Tree

The final paragraph of the September 9 *New York Times* story announcing the pardon reads:

> *Mr. Ford, after announcing the decision, went to the Burning Tree Country Club and played a round of golf. At the White House, switchboard operators said, "angry calls, heavy and constant," began jamming the boards soon after Mr. Ford's announcement.*

Typical of Ford, he had made his decision and moved on. The problem was, much of the country wasn't ready to go with him. Heading out to the golf course was just plain bad optics, a flashpoint. (Note to all future presidents: save your golf for days that you don't declare wars, sign laws that raise taxes, or hand out pardons to disgraced former presidents.)

The criticism of Ford was withering, some going so far as to accuse him of making a deal with Nixon prior to his resignation—in essence implying that Ford had bought the presidency with the promise of a pardon. His approval rating dropped from 71 percent to 49 percent. There is no doubt that the decision cost him votes in 1976. History, however, would judge his actions differently.

Bob Woodward and Carl Bernstein, the two young *Washington Post* reporters who broke open the Watergate story, were, at the time, both vehemently opposed to the pardon. Decades later, their views changed dramatically. Bernstein has said "it was the right thing to do," and Woodward called it "an act of courage."

In 2001, when Ford received the Profile in Courage Award at the John F. Kennedy Library, Senator Edward Kennedy told the audience: "I was one of those who spoke out against his action then. But time has a way of clarifying past events, and now we see that President Ford was right. His courage and dedication to our country made it possible for us to begin the process of healing and put the tragedy of Watergate behind us. I now fully realize there was no deal between Ford and Nixon, that Ford would pardon Nixon if Nixon resigned so that Ford would become president."

Sitting in the room that day, I thought that was a classy move on Ted's part.

But back in 1974, the healing process was proving to be painful. America just couldn't seem to come to grips with its recent past. The echoes of the battles and bombing runs in Southeast Asia and of the riots in our cities continued to reverberate. The United States had withdrawn its troops from Vietnam in the spring of 1973, and, in his speech to the VFW, Ford had begun the conversation about providing amnesty to those who had refused to serve there. But the wound continued to fester.

Over 58,000 Americans had died or gone missing defending our country's allies in South Vietnam. But now North Vietnam, with the support of China and others, was pressing its advantage. Ford and America faced a terrible question: Had all those lives been lost in vain? The Vietnam experience would shape our politics and our culture, the way we looked at ourselves and at the world, for decades to come. Just as it had fundamentally altered my life—and millions of other lives. Vietnam was the foreign body that changed our trajectory forever.

It was the war that wouldn't go away. If there was one thing that didn't die in Vietnam, it was irony. This theater of war had become a theater of the absurd.

That truth brings to mind something golfing great Jack Nicklaus told me years later at the Jerry Ford Invitational—a pro-am tournament hosted by former president Ford from the late seventies into the nineties. Given the opportunity to play with Jack, I made a point of asking for his advice every chance I got. On one of my shots, I delivered a direct hit into a greenside bunker, the ball plugging in the sand. I turned to Nicklaus and asked him what I should do. He looked down at the ball, then at me, and said:

"Just get out."

The wisest advice I've ever gotten: You're in a fix? *Just get out.*

Secret War

In June 1967, Secretary of Defense Robert McNamara commissioned a top-secret project titled *Report of the Office of the Secretary of Defense Vietnam Task Force.* Eighteen months later, five days before Nixon's inauguration, the Vietnam Study Task Force published fifteen copies of its report, each comprised of forty-seven volumes containing three thousand pages of historical analysis and four thousand pages of original government documents. Among the task force's many findings:

The primary motivation behind the increasing involvement of the United States in Southeast Asia was not to protect a friend—South Vietnam—but to contain a foe—China.

The United States government and military in essence created South Vietnam and actively interfered in its internal affairs—including sanctioning the overthrow of its president, Ngo Dinh Diem, in 1963.

Unlike the aerial assault on industrial complexes in Europe and Japan during the Second World War, the intensive bombing of North Vietnam—largely a rural country—had little or no impact on the enemy's will to fight.

A principal rationale for the continuing involvement in the war was to avoid a humiliating US defeat.

Two copies of the report went to the RAND Corporation, a think tank that had taken part in the project. Among its employees who had worked on the study was a military analyst and former first lieutenant in the United States infantry named Daniel Ellsberg. Increasingly opposed to the war and active in the anti-war movement, Ellsberg believed the American public had a right to see the report. To that end, he photocopied it, and in the winter and spring of 1971 started releasing portions of the forty-seven volumes to the *New York Times*.

In June 1971, the *Times* began to publish the Pentagon Papers. In the United States, the tide was already turning against the war, but the gravity of the report turned the tide into a tidal wave.

The release of the Pentagon Papers had a direct impact on my life and future. The Nixon White House, far more concerned by the leak of the Papers than by their content, created a covert Special Investigations Unit, The Plumbers, to plug the leak. In an effort to discredit Ellsberg, the Unit broke into his psychiatrist's office seeking dirt on him. The Plumbers later also broke into the Watergate. As President Nixon's White House chief of staff, H. R. Haldeman, later wrote: "Without the Vietnam war there would have been no Watergate." Without Watergate there would have been no President Ford, and without a Ford presidency, I never would have met, let alone worked for, the person who—aside from my mother and father—had the most profound impact on my life—Gerald Ford.

3

Hot, Cold, and Getting Warmer

Battle on Another Front

Nixon had left the building. Ford's pardon had swept the halls clear of him. The man—and the judgment of him—now belonged to history. Tying up loose ends, Ford's team had exiled Nixon's chief of staff, General Haig, to Europe to take command of NATO. It was Ford's White House now. And Ford's mess. His administration faced a daunting to-do list: find a way to tie off the festering wound that was Vietnam, contain the Soviets and corral the Chinese, prevent the oil crisis from strangling the economy, and stop inflation before it crushed the middle class.

No one was better suited for the challenges that lay ahead than President Ford. Just as he had back in the day, playing center for the national champion University of Michigan football team, he was ready to plant his feet, hold the line, and take on the world. But one issue caught him off guard, and like a sucker punch it made his knees buckle. It was the first of two great challenges he faced with the love of his life—two great challenges that, in the way the Fords responded to them, are perhaps the greatest legacies of his presidency.

On Friday, September 27, 1974, more than eight hundred of America's top minds—and biggest egos—gathered at the Washington Hilton Hotel. Captains of industry and union leaders, college professors and advertising executives, heavyweights from the worlds of politics, Wall Street, real estate, journalism, medicine, transportation, and agriculture—all coming together at the president's behest to participate in a national conference on inflation. Inflation had laid siege to the US dollar, and Ford brought out the big guns to fight it.

But even as many of America's brightest lights assembled at the Hilton that weekend, a dark shadow loomed over the president. The day before, on Thursday, during a routine examination at Walter Reed Army Hospital, doctors had discovered a lump in First Lady Betty Ford's breast. Friday evening she checked into the Bethesda Naval Medical Center. Early the next morning, Saturday, surgeons removed the nodule, and a biopsy confirmed that it was malignant. She had breast cancer. Wasting no time, they performed a mastectomy, removing her right breast, the underlying pectoral muscles, and the lymph-bearing tissue under her right arm.

They say tough guys don't cry. *They* are dead wrong. I first learned this from my father, who cried without shame on numerous occasions—and he was twice as strong and twice as dangerous as any dry-eyed challenger. During my time in the army and in Vietnam, I had been around some pretty rough, tough guys—but none tougher than Gerald Ford. (The one person tougher than him was his wife—I'll have lots more to say about her later.) When he stood up before the delegates that Saturday to reveal what the first lady had just gone through, there were tears in his eyes and a quiver in his voice. Ford was man enough to cry in public—in front of the cameras, in front of the entire country. Because before he was president, Ford was a son, a husband, and a father. Men might rule the world, but in his book, it was women who made it go round.

The Man Who Wouldn't Be King

On July 14, 1913, in Omaha, Nebraska, the president came into the world as a King—named after his biological father, Leslie Lynch King. But neither the name nor the father would stick. Weeks after the boy was born, his mother, Dorothy Gardner, bundled him up and fled to her parents' home in Grand Rapids, Michigan. It was a critical, courageous move, saving herself and her infant son from King—a wife-beating alcoholic who had threatened to kill them both with a kitchen knife.

Ford's mother divorced King and set out to make a life in this new town. She met and later married the owner of a local paint store—Gerald Rudolff Ford. Expunging her first husband from her life and her family, she renamed her son for the man who would be a father to him. Thus, a King became a Ford. Young Gerald didn't learn about his biological father until he was in high school, but just as, later on, the disgraced figure of Nixon would dog the early days of Ford's presidency, so did the shadow of his deadbeat dad loom over his college years.

Ford began his studies at the University of Michigan in the middle of the Great Depression. Times were tough, and his mom asked the court to increase King's monthly child support payments to help cover her son's tuition. The judge agreed, but the well-heeled King refused to pay a dime.

Ford waited on tables, washed dishes, did whatever he had to do to get by, the legal dispute dragging on for years. It was left to him, the great conciliator, to mediate, to act as peacemaker between King and his mother. Ford didn't care about the money. When, at last, he arranged a settlement, and King sent him a check, Ford passed it on to his mom. He said that she was the one who had suffered at King's hand, and so she deserved the money. All he wanted to do was get the man out of his mother's life.

During my time at Ford's side, both in the White House and in the years after, I saw the enormous respect he had for women. It was an old-fashioned type of respect, but it was pure, natural, and ever-present. He

greeted all women with an open mind, valuing their opinions as much as
he did their company. Even my own mom, given the opportunity, offered
counsel to the president.

Whenever Ford got word that some staff person's mother was visiting
the White House, all business would come to a halt as she—suddenly the
second most important person in the building—was escorted into the Oval
Office for a face-to-face with the POTUS. For my mom, it was heaven, her
chance to speak truth to power—and to me in the bargain. The president
quickly came out from behind his desk to take her hand and praise her son
to the skies. He told her how lucky he was to have me working for him,
what a wonderful job I was doing, and so forth—all the things a good boss
says to the mother of one of his employees.

"Well," she replied, nodding her head, looking up at him and over at
me, giving us the mom look, "both of you should travel less. Stay at home
more." And like that, she became the mother-in-chief, rendering the leader
of the free world momentarily speechless. Not that her advice was off
target. I couldn't speak for the president but staying at home more often
probably would have done me—and my marriage—a world of good. As
for the commander in chief, he finally managed to promise that he would
take her suggestion under advisement.

"Mom," I said, "don't you think we should be going?"

Partners

Ford's respect for women began with the relationship he had with his
mother. And that respect found its reward when Elizabeth (Betty) Warren
danced into his life. But she wasn't his first love. That distinction belonged
to Phyllis Brown, whom Ford had met while attending Yale Law School.
It was, by all accounts, a torrid affair.

The daughter of a Lewiston, Maine, department store owner, Phyllis was blond, beautiful, and athletic. When a photographer bumped into her on the ski slopes, instead of offering her an apology, he offered her a job. Thus began her long and successful career as a model. Through her connections, Jerry discovered that he, too, was good-looking enough to make a few dollars as a model. The two of them appeared together on the cover of *Cosmopolitan* magazine and in a spread in *Look* magazine.

Phyllis considered herself an eastern sophisticate, and she made it her business to introduce her handsome hayseed from the Midwest to the culture and nightlife of New York City. But after four years with Phyllis—Ford had finished with Yale—he was already beginning to contemplate a life in public service and politics. He knew that he belonged in Michigan, and that Phyllis didn't. She lived and breathed Manhattan—and so they parted ways.

In 1941, Ford returned to Grand Rapids to practice law—a career move interrupted by the Japanese when they bombed Pearl Harbor on December 7. Ford went to war. He enlisted in the navy, joining what newsman Tom Brokaw later dubbed America's "Greatest Generation." Ten battle stars and four years later, Ford returned from the South Pacific to dive back into the law. A social animal, he also began to cultivate relationships in and around Grand Rapids that would smooth his entrance into the political arena. But one critical relationship eluded him.

Ford was thirty-four years old when his mother (who else?) suggested that, as wonderful as it was that he was building such a nice career, it was time for him to cultivate a personal life as well. In other words: *Jerry, get yourself a girl and start a family.* Enter Betty Warren, professional dancer and fashion coordinator at a local department store. Just as she was not Ford's first love, neither was he hers. Betty was in the middle of a divorce when they first met. As many of us can attest from personal experience, the first time is not always a charm (in my case, neither was the second, third, or fourth), but Jerry and his future wife, Betty, turned out to be made for each other.

Fittingly, the Fords spent their honeymoon, during his first run for office, on the campaign trail—a trail that would lead them to the suburbs of Washington, and, down the road, to the White House, bringing four children into the world on the way. They were partners in politics as well as in life, and they never let their disagreements—Betty was far more liberal on social issues than her husband—get in the way of their mutual love, respect, and affection.

When Ford called Betty *his better half,* he was being neither glib nor face-tious. They had become a part of each other, which was why, standing in the ballroom of the Washington Hilton Hotel, before America's political, business, and cultural elite, Ford's eyes welled up and his voice cracked when he shared the news of the first lady's mastectomy. He later said that the night before the operation had been the loneliest of his life. The most powerful man in the world was powerless in a confrontation with his wife's breast cancer. Betty, on the other hand, was empowered by it. She found her voice.

I had been with the Fords for a little over six weeks, and now, for the first time, I witnessed what Gerald Ford must have seen all along: Betty's courage, strength, and sense of purpose. Before her operation, breast cancer and the mastectomies that followed had been a woman's dark secret, often a source of shame—a subject to be whispered about in doctors' offices if discussed at all.

Betty brought the cancer out of the closet, talking about it openly with the press and the public. She transformed fear and humiliation into hope and healing. Across the country, the number of women seeking mammo-grams rose exponentially. Although impossible to measure, it's likely that Betty Ford's action and candor in the face of the disease saved thousands of lives.

In an interview with the *Washington Post,* the first lady said that she and the president wanted to bring to the White House "the same feeling that we have had as a family, a feeling of unity and harmony and warmth." Although I had been with the Fords for only a very short time, I already began to sense that, yes, sure, this was my job, but it was becoming something more. Coming into work every day, no matter what crisis we were facing, I, too, felt that *unity and harmony and warmth* that Betty Ford described in the White House. The Fords didn't pay political lip service to family values; they demonstrated, through the lives they lived, the value of family.

Partners Part II

Back in August, Ford had made his first official decision as president. He announced that Nixon's secretary of state would continue in that capacity in his administration. A former professor at Harvard, Henry Kissinger was our point man overseas—in the Middle East, Southeast Asia, China, the Soviet Union, and everyplace in between. Wherever America had a seat at the table, he was there to preserve and protect the national interest. The stakes were astronomical—and Kissinger was our best poker player.

Ford had first crossed paths with his future secretary of state in 1958 when he was an inconspicuous Michigan congressman on the Defense Appropriations Subcommittee. Kissinger had invited the congressman to be a guest lecturer at Harvard's Defense Studies Program. Ford enjoyed the experience and, meeting Kissinger, was convinced that the professor was destined for great things. Kissinger, sharing that conviction, actively cultivated connections with government insiders like Ford. This mutual regard would only grow stronger in the decades to come.

In the years following Ford's lecture, the two men stayed in touch—a relationship of professional expediency that developed into a personal friendship. Both men had bright futures. Ford's star rose in Congress, his sights set on becoming Speaker of the House. Kissinger, through his writing and his work for Governor Rockefeller and Presidents Kennedy and Johnson, had his eye trained on the power centers of both Washington and New York.

Gerald Ford, the small-town Midwestern football player and lawyer, did not seek the presidency; it sought him. Henry Kissinger, the Eastern European immigrant, knew exactly what he wanted and went after it; he became secretary of state through the sheer force of his intelligence and ambition. The two of them couldn't have been more different, or more alike—each, in his own way, as American as apple pie. They complemented each other perfectly.

Their mutual respect and admiration jelled during the transition from Nixon's presidency to that of Ford. Ford recognized Kissinger's brilliance and appreciated his approach to foreign policy—driven not by ideology or special interests, but by the furtherance of *American* interests. Kissinger, for his part, valued Ford's decisiveness, candor, and inner peace—a welcome departure from the inner demons that drove Nixon.

Devious. Insecure. Arrogant. Distrusting. Hypersensitive. Hungry for fame. Kissinger could—and had been—all those things. But he could also be charming, creative, self-deprecating, and compassionate, with an unbelievable sense of humor and an uncanny sense of when to use it. He was in short, a complicated man. And with reason. He led a complicated life.

As a boy in Nazi Germany, young Kissinger would be beaten up for simply admitting who and what he was: Jewish. After immigrating to America, the thickly accented adolescent learned to adapt, chameleonlike, to a loud and liberating new culture in the streets of New York. As a soldier in the US Army, he returned to Germany, the land of his birth, where many of his relatives had perished in concentration camps. That was followed by Harvard, where the competition for tenure could put mud wrestlers to shame. And then Kissinger descended into the snake pit that was the Nixon White House. With a biography and background like that, it's no wonder that he brought a degree of deviousness and insecurity to the table.

The vagaries of history had brought Ford and Kissinger together, at the pinnacle of American power, at this critical time. The first great test of their partnership would come soon thereafter—not in the White House, but in a cold, gray, rusting city over six thousand miles away.

Breaking the Ice

President Ford didn't take my mom's advice, and neither did I. That fall we were both on the road and in the air, away from home far more than my mother would have liked.

The midterm elections were coming up on November 5, and Ford felt compelled to crisscross the country, playing the traveling salesman—as every president must during the political season—promoting and selling Republican candidates. But the public wasn't buying. The GOP didn't stand an ice cube's chance in hell in 1974. Watergate nearly killed the party; soaring inflation, the energy crisis, and the lingering ghosts of the Vietnam War were all accomplices.

The Democratic Party added to both of its majorities in Congress, taking forty-nine seats from the Republicans in the House of Representatives and four in the Senate. Ford had gamely fought a losing battle. But the season was not a total loss. He did achieve a victory that November—in a place where not a single US citizen, Democrat or Republican, lived.

On Sunday, November 17, President Ford took off in Air Force One on an eight-day journey—first stop, Anchorage, Alaska, then on to Japan, South Korea, and finally Vladivostok, the Far Eastern Russian city in the extreme southeastern corner of the Soviet Union. There, he would meet for the first time with the Soviet leader General Secretary Leonid Brezhnev. The rendezvous between the two heads of state had been thirty years in the making.

On August 6, 1945, at 8:15 in the morning (Hiroshima time), a United States Army Air Force B-29 bomber dropped and detonated the atomic bomb designated Little Boy over the Japanese city. It was the dark, white-hot closing act of the Second World War and the fearsome opening salvo of what came to be known as the Cold War. Over the next several decades, the United States and the Soviet Union engaged in a global, existential game of chicken—a mine-is-bigger-than-yours competition for supremacy in nuclear armaments.

By the 1950s, the race to create and accumulate nuclear warheads, along with the devices to deliver them, had reached such epic proportions that each side possessed the capacity to wipe the other off the face of the Earth. It gave rise to the doctrine of mutually assured destruction—MAD for short. The theory was, the more nuclear weapons each side had, the less likely either was to use them. A nuclear attack on your enemy would be suicidal. In other words: *You turn my country into a vast radioactive wasteland, I'll rain holy hell down on yours.* Turnabout is fair play. Not hardly—turnabout would have amounted to the end of the world as we know it.

I'm no expert—I only carried the nuclear codes, I didn't decide how or when to use them—but there are clearly several holes in the MAD theory of nuclear deterrence. First of all, it's a theory based on rational thinking. If history tells us anything, it's that humans don't always act in a rational way. We can be stupid, impulsive, on occasion evil, and sometimes we just make mistakes in judgment. Another problem, which became an issue by the end of the 1960s, was money. If your survival depends on keeping up with the Joneses, then every time they get a bigger, better bomb or submarine, you have to get one, too.

Both superpowers faced the same reality: The arms race could not be sustained. It simply cost too much. And the only way to stop it, or at least slow it down, was for these two adversaries—the United States and the Soviet Union—to sit down at the same table and agree to set limits. In 1969 the Strategic Arms Limitation Talks (SALT) began to do just that, and three years later Nixon famously traveled to Moscow to meet with Brezhnev. The Cold War was far from over, but the ice had been broken.

Now, it was up to President Ford to continue the thawing-out process in Vladivostok. Progress would depend on the degree to which these two party loyalists—the Republican Ford and the Communist Brezhnev—warmed to each other.

Black Marble

The Boeing VC-137C SAM 26000, delivered to the US Air Force in 1962, was the first jet aircraft built specifically for use by the president of the United States. Over the years, it had carried more than its share of historical presidential baggage.

On November 22, 1963, as Air Force One, it flew President John F. Kennedy and First Lady Jacqueline Kennedy to Dallas's Love Field. Hours later, after Kennedy was assassinated, Lyndon Johnson stood in the plane's cabin—next to Jackie in her bloodied pink dress—to be sworn in; it then bore the new president and JFK's body back to Washington. In the next decade, it would transport Johnson to Vietnam and later bring Nixon to China and the Soviet Union.

By 1974, the SAM 26000 had become the president's backup aircraft, and when, on Sunday, November 10, it touched down at Vozdvizhenka, the sprawling Soviet air base near Vladivostok, no president was on board. I was.

Ford was scheduled to arrive for his talks with Brezhnev in thirteen days, on November 23, and I was there as part of the pre-advance team. It consisted of the White House chief of protocol, the appointments secretary to the president, a special assistant to the president; members of the Secret Service, the State Department, the White House Communications Agency, the press office, and the National Security Agency; a presidential physician, the White House food coordinator, and a helicopter pilot, as well as several people I'd never seen before and whose roles were a mystery to me. My guess: they were in intelligence. A trip such as this would not be undertaken without a few CIA agents tagging along for the ride—and, if that's who they were, I'm sure the Soviets knew more about them than I did. It was the job of the White House advance office to pull this large entourage together.

The pre-advance team's mission was to begin the process of creating a home away from home—a White House away from the White House—for the president to settle into once here. We were part of that huge, intricate, mostly invisible apparatus that preceded, surrounded, and moved with the commander in chief whenever he traveled.

On the helicopter ride from the air base to the Okeanskaya Sanatorium—site of the upcoming summit meeting—I couldn't help but notice that there were some issues we would need to address. Oil leaking from the aircraft being one. I kept my counsel until we reached our destination and we were out of earshot of the Soviets. Others on our team had also observed the leaks, and we reached out, on a secure line, to Scowcroft in Washington, advising that the president not be allowed on any Soviet helicopters. Scowcroft worked his magic: Ford would be transported to the spa on the more controlled environment of a train.

While on the flight, we were admonished by our Soviet handlers not to take photographs. I'm not sure how images of the snowy landscape, the small villages and old farmhouses, and the forests of pine and white birch that we flew over would compromise Soviet security, but we did as we were told. The warning served as a reminder that we were not on friendly ground—and of the fraught and complicated task faced by Ford and Brezhnev. Out here on the edge of the world, in the middle of nowhere, the two leaders would be at the center of everything.

Looking down at the countryside, I was awestruck. This was the Soviet Union—Russia—land of Peter the Great, Tolstoy, and Lenin. Our helicopter was bound for the outskirts of Vladivostok, terminus of the Trans-Siberian Railway, home port of the Soviet Pacific Fleet, a city officially closed to foreigners. The name of the place alone—like Casablanca or Istanbul—evoked an exotic world of mystery, intrigue, and romance—this job was taking me places.

But then we came to the spa at Okeanskaya—comprised of a large white stone building surrounded by fields and small wooden cottages. There was no mystery or romance here, just peeling paint on the walls and debris piled in the corners—the whole complex in utter disrepair. Gray and decaying, with corruption evident everywhere: Soviet Communist Russia in a nutshell.

Our counterparts from Moscow, Brezhnev's advance team, gave us the grand tour—there was virtually no heat, it was freezing, the walls were cracked, and chunks of concrete littered the hallways—and then they brought us to the natatorium.

The Soviets knew that Ford liked to swim. "Here," one of them said with a straight face, "is a pool for your president." Tiles had fallen off the walls, and dirt encrusted the floor. This pool had clearly not held water for years, and there was no way the Secret Service was ever going to let Ford get near this hole in the ground. Not wanting to be rude to our hosts, we just nodded our heads and carried on with the tour. But the next day, the Soviet hammer and sickle were brought to bear.

In came the machinery, the material, and the men to work it. Heavy equipment and skilled laborers, they went to work on the pool—and the heating system and hallways. For ten days straight, sixteen hours a day, they bent that place to their will. By the end of those ten days, that swimming pool was a work of art, the mosaic on its walls and floor replaced and restored, inch by inch, tile by tile.

I marveled at the time and energy spent on the pool. When huge, expensive pieces of equipment broke down in the subzero temperatures, they'd just bring in more—all of this for Ford, who would be here for fewer than forty-eight hours and who might find fifteen minutes, at most, to swim a few laps. I later said to Brent Scowcroft how much of a waste it seemed to me, a gross misallocation of resources.

Scowcroft said, "You're looking but you're not seeing. When the Russians decide to do something, they do it."

"Imagine," Scowcroft went on, "that they want a perfect cube of black marble. They'll get a huge block of marble and start chipping away at it, day after day, not stopping until they have a perfect cube. But if one worker slips up and chips off a corner, they throw that imperfect cube away, get themselves another block of marble, and start all over again. You ask about the waste, but it's the wrong question. What you should be asking is: Dear God, how many pieces of marble do they have?"

It was a teaching moment—Scowcroft telling me that, while technologically we had a distinct advantage over the Soviets, they had considerably more resources than we did, whether it's marble, or oil, or workers to pull it out of the ground. The parable continues to resonate in our own time. Today's swimming pool, today's cube of black marble, is the United States election: the Russians will continue to hack away at it—tirelessly and relentlessly—until they have shaped it to their liking.

Ford and Kissinger were negotiating for control over the proliferation of nuclear arms. Nowadays, the war is waged in cyberspace.

Fun and Games

The Russians weren't the only ones working long days. In most cases, when the president traveled, the pre-advance team would head out a couple of weeks ahead of him, take a few days to set things up, then head back to Washington. But most places weren't as decrepit and decayed as this spa was. The facilities at Okeanskaya were in such disrepair, and there was so much to be done—devising a workable electrical system, putting together a viable kitchen, securing the president's quarters—we decided to stay on for the full two weeks prior to his arrival. But it wasn't all work and no play.

Every afternoon, I'd organize a touch football game between our guys and the Soviet security people. But the word *touch* doesn't capture the spirit of those games. For a half hour each day, the Cold War turned hot out on the spa's abandoned clay tennis courts—a dozen grown men in T-shirts, in the bitter cold, tossing a pigskin around and banging the living hell out of each other. And the harder we hit those Russians, the more they seemed to like it, giving as good as they got.

As our hosts and counterparts, they took it upon themselves to keep us entertained, piling us into a bus and taking us into the city—to the circus or out to dinner. It was very instructive. One lesson I learned: when dining out in the far eastern Soviet Union, always order the chicken. Their cuisine—lots of raw fish—was not to my taste, but chicken is universal, and it's hard to mess up when you cook one.

The moral of the story: see the world, soak up the culture, order the chicken.

The Score

"I would rather travel thousands of miles for peace," President Ford said, "than take a single step toward war."

On November 22, after twelve days of hard labor, rough football, and lots of Siberian chicken, we were ready for the president at the far end of that journey. We had somehow carved out of that relic of a resort a secure, self-contained, fully customized environment—swimming pool and all—capable of handling a summit meeting between the two most powerful men on the planet. And that's when the blizzard hit—a foot of fresh snow blanketing the resort, the countryside, and the air base where the two leaders were scheduled to land.

It's hard to fathom the enormity of the Soviet (now Russian) landmass. Ford had a relatively short flight in from Japan. Brezhnev, on the other hand, had to traverse seven time zones—Moscow is closer to New York than it is to Vladivostok. We later learned that, because of the blizzard, several officials traveling with Brezhnev suggested moving the summit to a city that had dodged the storm, more than four hundred miles to the north.

The men and women of the Secret Service are about as cool, calm, and collected a bunch as you'll find anywhere in the world, but if this plan had gone live, I suspect that their collective heads would have exploded. It would have meant that we—the entire advance team—would have had to find a way to get to the new venue and then improvise there, in less than twenty-four hours, what we had painstakingly created and constructed, over the course of nearly two weeks, here at Okeanskaya.

Fortunately, saner Soviets prevailed, and the move was deep-sixed. Brezhnev's plane landed at an airfield to the north, and he completed the journey by train. Plows cleared a single airstrip at Vozdvizhenka, the same air base we had flown into, and early in the afternoon of Saturday, November 23, Air Force One touched down. We were in business.

There was no pomp and circumstance—the marching bands neutralized by the weather—but Brezhnev and his entourage were there on the tarmac to meet the president and his men. The first item on Brezhnev's agenda was Ford's coat. En route to the Far East, Air Force One had stopped to refuel in Alaska, where an old friend, a furrier, had given the president a wolfskin fur coat—perfect for this remote Russian outpost. Ford wasn't a flashy guy, but the fur stood out in this sea of black and gray overcoats. The Russian leader shook the president's hand and took an immediate liking to his coat, both men all smiles.

The train that brought them to Okeanskaya was luxurious in an Orient Express kind of way—with its curtained windows, caviar, and cognac. It brought Tsarist Russia and Dr. Zhivago to mind. Ford and Brezhnev, along with a small group of advisors, sat across from each other at a table in the main compartment. While the president and the general secretary talked sports—football and soccer—Kissinger ate, working his way through three

President Gerald R. Ford and Bob Barrett, White House Colonnade. *Courtesy of the Gerald R. Ford Presidential Library.*

ABOVE: President Gerald R. Ford and Maj. Barrett, military aide, at the Washington Hilton Hotel, Washington, DC. *Courtesy of the Gerald R. Ford Presidential Library.* BELOW: President Gerald R. Ford, Susan Ford, and Maj. Barrett in the Oval Office. *Courtesy of the Gerald R. Ford Presidential Library.*

Maj. Barrett (left), President Gerald R. Ford in a wolfskin coat and Russian wool cap, and the Secret Service on a trip to the USSR, prior to meeting with General Secretary Leonid Brezhnev. *Photo by David Hume Kennerly, courtesy of the Gerald R. Ford Presidential Library.*

ABOVE: Maj. Barrett and President Gerald R. Ford in the Oval Office prior to the Medal of Honor Presentation Ceremony. *Courtesy of the Gerald R. Ford Presidential Library.* BELOW: Maj. Barrett and Liberty, the first family's dog, in the Scheduling and Advance Office. *Courtesy of he Gerald R. Ford Presidential Library.*

ABOVE: Maj. Barrett on phone while traveling on Air Force One. *Courtesy of the Gerald R. Ford Presidential Library.* BELOW: President Gerald R. Ford and Maj. Barrett walking from Marine One, on the South Lawn, White House. *Courtesy of the Gerald R. Ford Presidential Library.*

Maj. Barrett and President Gerald R. Ford on the second floor of the White House prior to a dinner for the prime minister of the Netherlands. *Courtesy of the Gerald R. Ford Presidential Library.*

Pope Paul VI and Maj. Barrett, Vatican City, Rome, Italy. *Courtesy of the Gerald R. Ford Presidential Library.*

Maj. Barrett (second from left) and President Gerald R. Ford on a campaign trip arriving at Los Angeles International Airport. Barrett is carrying the "nuclear football." *Courtesy of the Gerald R. Ford Presidential Library/Barrett Family Archives.*

ABOVE: Maj. Barrett holding an umbrella for President Gerald R. Ford at the International Economic Summit in Rambouillet, France. *Courtesy of the Gerald R. Ford Presidential Library.* BELOW: Barrett and President Ford walking in Vail, CO. *Courtesy of the Barrett Family Archives.*

ABOVE: President Gerald R. Ford and Maj. Robert E. Barrett shaking hands after presenting the Legion of Merit Medal. *Courtesy of the Barrett Family Archives.* LEFT: Gerald and Betty Ford in flight. *Courtesy of the Barrett Family Archives.*

ABOVE: Barrett, 1st Cavalry Division, Vietnam. *Courtesy of the Barrett Family Archives.* LEFT: Barrett and Mrs. Betty Ford dancing. *Courtesy of the Barrett Family Archives.*

To all who shall see these presents, greeting:

In recognition of his ability and patriotism

Robert E. Barrett
of
Vail, Colorado

is hereby appointed Civilian Aide to the Secretary of the Army to serve as such until 12 April 1985 . He shall cooperate with the Department of the Army in such manner as to enhance the relationship between the United States Army and the civilian community.

ABOVE: Robert E. Barrett's Civilian Aide to the Secretary of the Army certificate. *Courtesy of the Barrett Family Archives.* BELOW: Gerald R. Ford and Bob Barrett. *Courtesy of the Barrett Family Archives.*

Taking notes. *Courtesy of the Barrett Family Archives.*

Bob Barrett and Henry Kissinger. *Courtesy of the Barrett Family Archives.*

ABOVE: Control car in the motorcade. BELOW: First Lady Betty Ford and Maj. Barrett. *Courtesy of the Barrett Family Archives.*

President Gerald R. Ford and Leonid Brezhnev, General Secretary of the Communist Party of the USSR, meeting in Vladivostok, USSR, to sign a joint communiqué on the limitation of strategic offensive arms. *Courtesy of the Gerald R. Ford Presidential Library/Barrett Family Archive.*

The arrival ceremony at the Quirinale Palace, the residence of the president of Italy. President Leone, President Ford, and Maj. Barrett (behind Ford) walking on a red carpet past the Mounted Honor Guard in Rome, Italy. *Courtesy of the Barrett Family Archives.*

ABOVE: Former U.S. President Gerald R. Ford and Chief of Staff Robert Barrett talk on an airplane enroute to Syria during Ford's 1979 Mideast Tour. *Photo by David Hume Kennerly. Credit: Getty Images.* BELOW: John Purcell, dear friend of President Ford, with Gerald Ford, in Vail, Colorado. *Courtesy of the Barret Family Archives.*

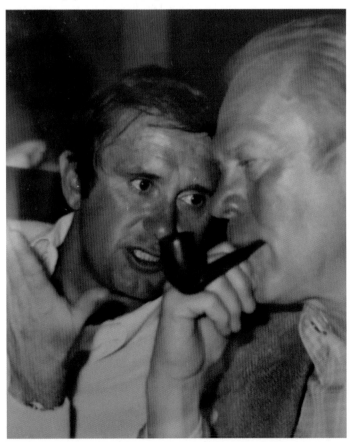

plates of pastries. He had a habit of eating when anxious or on edge, and this was *his* show after all.

Sometime after four, Brezhnev's black limousine, with Soviet and American flags flapping, conveyed the two leaders from the train to the compound, border guards in suede Cossack coats and black leather boots posted at close intervals along the route. Arriving at Ford's dacha, Brezhnev accompanied the president into the entrance hall, where they kicked off the summit with champagne—alcohol, in all its forms, one of the basic food groups in Russia.

After the toast, Ford stepped outside to shake Brezhnev's hand and see him off. He then turned to the press pool and said, "Throw a snowball at Kennerly."

David Hume Kennerly was Ford's official photographer and unofficial prankster, cutup, and wiseass. He was the guy who could get away with anything. Like the time the president planned a working weekend at Camp David, and Kennerly informed the Secret Service that he was bringing a girlfriend along with him.

They told him, "No way, you can't do that."

So Kennerly went to Ford, who said, "I can't wait to meet her."

I took an instant liking to David, and over the next couple of years some of his immunity from presidential prosecution rubbed off on me. He, Terry O'Donnell, Ford's personal aid, and I became known as the Three Muske-teers. Before coming to the White House, Kennerly was a *Time* magazine photographer doing fearless work in Vietnam. He could walk into the Oval Office at any time. It didn't matter who was in with the president.

I would see him go up to Nell Yates (the president's secretary, the keeper of the gate) and say, "What's going on, Nell?"

"He's in with Kissinger and Scowcroft." Or Maggie Thatcher, or anyone else on the planet. Dave would go straight in. Ford wouldn't even look up, and he and his guest would typically continue whatever they were talking about.

Ford loved Dave. And Dave loved more women than anyone else in DC. I learned the greatest pickup line in the world from Dave:

"How would you like to meet the president?"

The formal talks between Ford and Brezhnev began after six and were scheduled to go for about two hours. They lasted until well past midnight. Brezhnev had the power to make decisions but still often left the room to confer with the Politburo back in Moscow. Several times the Americans went out as well, not to make phone calls, but to huddle outside in the deep freeze, figuring that anyplace in the compound that had walls would also have listening devices. The chill out in the courtyard gave physical proof of the vital importance of negotiation with the Soviets. No one—Napoleon and Hitler among them—had ever successfully invaded Russia. It was too goddamned cold. Frostbite was its last line of defense.

That Saturday evening was a long, tough night of confrontation, negotiation, and horse-trading as the two sides lobbed long-range bombers, submarines, MIRVs (multiple warheads), and missile launchers across the table at each other. Remarkably, by the end of the meeting, an agreement had been put into place—one that was a clear victory for the United States. Ford, Kissinger, and all their senior aides went to bed happy, knowing that their hard work and long trip had paid off.

Still, I contend that no one, not even Kissinger, had a tougher job that weekend than I did. I was tasked with conveying to the president the score of a football game—and not just any game but the *Michigan–Ohio State* football game. Or, as those in the know called it, THE GAME. And THE GAME was a war.

"Bob," Ford said as he went to his room for the night, "wake me at six with the score."

I didn't have to ask what score he meant. President Ford's blood ran Michigan Blue, where he had been an All-American and captain of the football team in the 1930s. At that time, Willie Woods was the only Black player on the team. Ford's senior year, Michigan's head coach got a letter from the head coach at Georgia Tech—the team Michigan was scheduled to play against in Atlanta:

We would appreciate it if you did not bring Willie Woods here to play in our upcoming game.

When Ford got wind of it, he went in to see the coach.

"If Willie doesn't play, I don't play," he said and walked back out.

The letter was withdrawn. Woods played. Michigan won.

But the news the next morning in Russia out of Columbus, Ohio, was not good, and I didn't much like the idea of poking the bear—the president being ninety-eight parts koala and two parts grizzly—first thing in the morning. But I had my orders. I woke him at exactly six o'clock, and he wasted no time: *What was the score?*

Twelve to ten, I said, and then tried to beat a quick retreat.

Not a chance.

Who had the twelve, he wanted to know.

The expression on my face—sadness? sympathy? fear?—said it all. I told him the Michigan kicker had missed a short field goal as time ran out. Ford expressed his disappointment, said he felt sorry for the Michigan kid, and, fortunately for me, decided not to shoot the messenger.

Sunday's meeting started at ten and lasted only two hours. Little was accomplished, but Ford was euphoric from the previous night's meeting. The high point of the Sunday morning session came during a break when Brezhnev proudly presented Ford with an intricate woodcarving, a kind of jigsaw puzzle portrait of the president. Ford stepped outside the conference room and held the carving up for a group of us to see. Kennerly, clicking away and capturing the moment for posterity, said, "Would you look at that. They gave you a picture of Frank Sinatra."

Ford was not amused. But what was he going to do? He might have momentarily considered throwing Kennerly out of Air Force One at

35,000 feet, but he just sighed. It was just Kennerly being Kennerly. I know I stifled a laugh, and I wasn't alone—because damn if the portrait in wood wasn't the spitting image of Old Blue Eyes.

Later that evening Ford improvised a gift for Brezhnev. After giving the president a driving tour of Vladivostok, Brezhnev accompanied him on the train back to the air base. On the tarmac they shook hands and gave each other a bear hug. Ford started up the stairs to Air Force One, stopped, and came back down. He took off the wolfskin fur coat and handed it to Brezhnev. It was a priceless moment for both men, a move right out of the Russian playbook—the diplomatic equivalent of a pure black cube of marble.

The Bull and the Foxe

Several hours after midnight, on the morning of October 7, 1974, a black Lincoln Continental sped through the streets of Washington, its headlights off. A couple of Federal Park cops spotted the car and chased it down, pulling it over halfway between the Washington Monument and the Jefferson Memorial. The driver's-side rear door of the Lincoln opened and a short, drunken man with a bloody nose and scratches on his cheek stepped out, threatening to have the policemen's badges. Seconds later, a young woman in high heels leaped out the opposite side of the car and threw herself into the Tidal Basin.

The woman, who was fished out of the water by one of the officers, was a stripper who went by the stage name Fanne Foxe, "the Argentine Firecracker." The man with the bleeding face was Wilbur Mills, chairman of the House Ways and Means Committee, and—up until that night—perhaps the second most powerful man in Washington. Within several months, however, his chairmanship was gone. As was his power. Fanne's leap into the Basin—and its aftermath—was a sign of the times.

Powerful politicians behaving badly was nothing new in Washington. What *was* new was the press reporting it. Drinking, womanizing, all sorts of unbecoming conduct used to get a wink from reporters instead of a headline. Those days were gone. In the aftermath of the Pentagon Papers and Watergate, trust in America's institutions—government, military, and business—crashed. Now, when the press dug into a story, it dug deep, and private lives were an integral part of the narrative.

Today the situation has spun out of control. Fox, CNN, and MSNBC, with their twenty-four-hour news cycles, compete for ratings and for dollars—the more lurid and sensational the story, the better. And as anyone with a cell phone (meaning everyone) is a "journalist" and "videographer," there's no such thing as privacy anymore.

Back in 1974, reacting to the Wilbur Mills embarrassment and to the climate of the times, Congress wrested authority away from a few back-room power brokers. As a result, Ford had to contend with an evolving calculus of power in Washington. Negotiating with Brezhnev turned out to be easier than working with his own Congress.

A decade earlier, if President Johnson wanted to move some legislation through Congress, he could reach out to four, five, maybe half a dozen members of the House—bulls like Wilbur Mills. But now the old bulls were being put out to pasture, their power dispersed among a membership that was more reflective of a fractured and polarized country.

I believe openness in government is a good thing. But today it has gone to extremes. Politics has gone tribal; disagreements in policy lead to grandstanding, name-calling, Twitter wars, and government shutdowns. There are times when legislators should just shut up, walk away from the microphone, and legislate.

Congress killed the accords that Ford had reached with Brezhnev in Vladivostok. The Right thought the deal went too far; the Left complained that it didn't go far enough. In my book, that means that the agreement, like Goldilocks's porridge, was not too hot and not too cold, but *just right*.

Although the agreement was never signed, the relationship Ford forged with the Soviet leader would, over time, prove invaluable—most notably the following summer, in Helsinki.

Family Jewels

But summer was a long way away, and on the domestic front, the country was about to enter a winter of discontent.

Late in December the president, the first lady, their family, and some close friends assembled in Vail, Colorado—a small town built in Tyrolean style around a ski resort at Vail Mountain. In 1970 the Fords had purchased a three-bedroom walk-up in the center of town, directly above the Wicked West clothing store, and had been coming back there every winter since.

This, of course, was the first time they had come to Vail with an army of staff and reporters in tow. And this time, at the behest of the Secret Service, they would not be staying in a three-bedroom walk-up above a clothing store. This year they would celebrate Christmas and New Year's at a more elaborate—and more secure—seven-room chalet.

The press *loved* this assignment. To get away from Washington and go to a first-class resort on an expense account—nothing could be better. Ford had a very healthy relationship with them—he was forthcoming (the man couldn't lie), he was accessible, and he could take a joke as well as give one, even though it might be inadvertent. He loved the press, and they loved him. Journalistic icons like Helen Thomas and Tom Brokaw became good friends with the president, and, as a satellite in orbit around him over the years, I became friends with them as well.

On another trip to Vail, Betty was in the bedroom unpacking. I was in the living room with the president. He devoured newspapers—every day he read at a minimum the *New York Times*, the *Times* of London, the *Washington Post*, the *LA Times*, and the *Palm Desert Post*, all cover to cover. I would pick up and leaf through whichever one he had just finished. So he was sitting there reading one of those papers with stacks all around him when Betty finally came and joined us in the room. It was the first time they had been together since she had been on *60 Minutes* with Morley Safer. Among other things, she said that *Roe vs. Wade*, the Supreme Court case granting women the right to abortion, was a "great" decision, that in all likelihood her kids had tried marijuana, and that she wouldn't be at all surprised if her eighteen-year-old daughter, Susan, had already had an affair.

It turned out that Betty Ford had set the evangelical right wing of the Republican Party on fire. The president was sitting there, his face hidden behind one of his morning papers, when she came in and asked:

"Jerry, did you see *60 Minutes* last night?"

"Uh, yeah, yeah, I saw it."

"Well, do you think it's going to cause you any problems politically?"

"No. Only if I wanted to get elected, Betty. Only if I wanted to get elected."

He never lowered the newspaper. President Ford was really a funny man. But it was only in that dry seeming lack of awareness that he was being funny that his humor showed. It was only when he actually tried to tell a joke that he failed miserably.

On that first trip to Vail, I didn't accompany the president on Air Force One, but I was in Colorado to meet him when he arrived. Vail was a working vacation for Ford, as it was for me. But it was also something more. My background—in academics, athletics, and the military—resonated with the president, as did my approach to work. I took my job seriously, but I never took myself too seriously. Simply put, my manner suited him. For whatever reason, Ford, the first lady, and their children took to me, and I was here in Vail not only as the president's military aide, but as his guest. He urged me to bring out my whole family, which I did.

Bev was ecstatic. She had made it clear recently that she believed we needed to spend more time together—both as a couple and as a family—and, as she saw it, ten days at a Rocky Mountain retreat was just the medicine for what ailed us. Also, Vail was an ideal environment for her. She loved to ski and socialize, a natural at both, equally at ease gliding down the slopes or into a cocktail party.

Ford, too, was in his element. For two hours a day, no matter what the temperature—even when Vail was colder than Vladivostok—he'd strap on the skis and head out, Secret Service agents spread out all over the mountain to maintain a perimeter. If he'd had it his way, he would have been out there from dawn to dusk, flying down the trails, icicles forming on his eyelashes. But his time was squeezed. The president had gotten out of Washington, but not away from it. There was no escaping its madness and mayhem; it had all flown west with him.

This was the headline—stretching across four columns in the Sunday *New York Times*—that Ford read on Air Force One as he made his way to Colorado:

HUGE C.I.A. OPERATION REPORTED IN U.S. AGAINST ANTIWAR FORCES, OTHER DISSIDENTS IN NIXON YEARS

Now *that* was a slippery slope.

The original idea for creating the Central Intelligence Agency—much like the formation of the Department of Homeland Security—grew out of a devastating attack on American soil: the failure of US intelligence services to coordinate signs warning of the attack on Pearl Harbor. But in the six years between the attack and the formal charter of the CIA, the world had changed, and so had the Agency's scope and mission.

President Truman saw it as a key element in the United States' new responsibility as a major global power. By law, the CIA would not only gather intelligence, it would also undertake clandestine operations abroad. The operations would be designed to counter and contain the Soviet menace. The key word was *abroad*. If the Agency had in fact operated domestically, as the *Times* had reported, then it was in clear violation of its charter—and yet another body blow to America's trust in its institutions.

We were in the middle of a decade—the 1970s—marked by conspiracy theories and paranoia. Movies such as *Three Days of the Condor* and *The Parallax View* depicted deep, dark, ultrasecret government agencies going after some of America's most popular—and best-looking—heroes: Robert Redford and Warren Beatty. If they were fair game, well, then nothing was sacred and no one was safe. Now here, in America's newspaper of record, was a headline that seemed to justify that paranoia. Pogo, in the funny papers, captured it best: *We have met the enemy and he is us.* For those fearful of the divisiveness created by today's political climate, it's helpful to remember that we've seen this movie before.

As far as the administration was concerned, there was nothing funny at all about the headline. Kissinger warned Ford that the story was "just the tip of the iceberg" and that if other operations were exposed "blood will flow." The secretary of state was referring to the "family jewels"—so-called inside the CIA because they were secrets so sensitive they had to remain locked up, never to see the light of day.

But secrets were not what they used to be. Other presidents, before Nixon, had taped their conversations, and other politicians, before Wilbur Mills, had gotten drunk and run around with young women who were not their wives. Washington hadn't changed, the times had. Now it was the CIA's turn to cough up its secrets. And it was a bloody mess.

The family jewels didn't sparkle. A quarter century of kidnappings and attempted assassinations overseas, infiltration of leftist groups, domestic spying and break-ins, surveillance of journalists, and tests on unwitting American civilians with drugs like LSD. As the revelations rose darkly to the surface, many clamored for an end to the CIA altogether. Ford was pressed to shut it down and lock it up for good.

The White House and the CIA have always had a love-hate relationship. Kennedy took the Agency's advice and paid for it at the Bay of Pigs. Johnson ignored its advice and paid for it in Southeast Asia. Nixon bullied the CIA into doing his bidding, and they all paid for it in Watergate. Most recently, Trump blasted the intelligence community, often casting it as his nemesis.

But for Ford, ending the Agency was not an option. He didn't want to throw out the baby with the bathwater. He knew that the CIA served a vital function; the trick was making sure it did not stray beyond its charter—in other words, finding a way to save the Agency from itself. He had to do for the CIA what he was already doing for the presidency.

Auld Lang Syne

Nineteen seventy-four had been a hell of a year. I had gone from a quiet post in the hinterlands, at the Army War College, to a White House in turmoil and under siege. I had watched the United States government descend into the belly of the beast—the republic facing its greatest crisis since the Civil War—and come out intact, strengthened by the crisis. And I had been embraced by a man and his family who would direct and shape my life for years to come.

There was plenty to celebrate on New Year's Eve. Bev and I spent it, along with some fifty other guests, at the Fords' mountain chalet. The president, in a blue turtleneck and a crimson blazer, worked the room, joking, shaking hands, relishing his role as host. The first lady, in a lemon-yellow dress, did the same. There were younger, hipper, richer people at the party, but the Fords were clearly the coolest couple in the room.

One of the traits I most admired about the president was that when he worked, he worked, and when he played, he played. He didn't obsess as LBJ had or brood like Nixon—and that last night of 1974, he was living in the moment.

"Give me the job of justice of the peace here," he quipped, "and I'll quit the presidency."

As midnight came and went, the party over, Vail giving way to Washington, I wondered if there was some wistful, wishful thinking in the
president's justice-of-the-peace joke. Nineteen seventy-five was looking
like it would be an awful lot like 1974. Millions of Americans were unem-
ployed, and those who had income found their money was devalued by the
continued rise of inflation. The energy crisis threatened to stall business and
make the coming winter a cold one in many homes. And two committees
in Congress announced investigations into the CIA.

Wherever Ford looked he saw confidence in the government and
economy eroding. On January 15, two weeks into the new year, he went
before the two houses of Congress, looked America in the eye, and
announced:

The state of the union is not good.

Of course, my problems didn't amount to a mosquito bite compared to
what the president and the country faced, but I couldn't help but reflect
that the words he spoke that night could as well have described the state
of my marriage. Vail had not been the cure that Bev had been seeking
for our relationship, and that holiday on the mountain would prove to be
one of the last merry Christmases and happy New Year's that my wife
and I would spend together.

A White Christmas

The world came to an end at 7:53 in the morning on April 30, 1975. It
wasn't my world anymore, but it had been at one time. The collapse had
been a long time coming, but it was in March of '75 that things began to fall
apart in earnest. Two years earlier, in the spring of 1973, the United States
military had pulled out of South Vietnam, leaving a hole in that country's

heart and economy. It was our part in a peace accord that Kissinger had negotiated in Paris. In exchange, North Vietnam had agreed to a ceasefire.

In reality, however, the fire never ceased, small battles continuing across the countryside. But now, in 1975, the North Vietnamese leadership decided to test America's resolve. They launched a major attack on the South, a clear violation of the Paris Peace Accords, to see how the United States would respond. Our only response was not to respond at all. American troops would not be sent back, there would be no more bombing runs, and the United States Treasury was closed for business. South Vietnam was on its own.

Fiercely loyal, President Ford thought it was a cardinal sin for the United States to abandon its ally. I thought the strain on him that spring was greater than any other time during his presidency—greater even than when he pardoned Nixon. The possible collapse of South Vietnam was a weight on his shoulders. But he had no recourse. Congress tied his hands.

He pleaded for more military aid, but Congress refused to allocate another nickel in cash or hardware to the South Vietnamese government. The American people, they argued, didn't have the stomach for any more fighting in Southeast Asia. And neither, it turned out, did the South Vietnamese Army.

Meeting little if any resistance, the North Vietnamese rolled across the countryside and into many of the cities formerly controlled by the South. Hundreds of thousands of retreating civilians and soldiers moved away from the advancing Communists in what came to be known as the "Convoy of Tears." Roads were littered with the boots and uniforms of soldiers who had abandoned the war to return to their families.

On March 29, when an American Boeing 727 landed in Danang to airlift refugees to Saigon, thousands of South Vietnamese on bicycles, on scooters, and on foot raced across the tarmac. Old women and children were pushed aside as members of an elite South Vietnamese military unit fought—and killed—for space on the plane. When the 727 finally managed to take off, some who had failed to get aboard clung to the undercarriage only to fall into the South China Sea.

Along the coast, refugees packed onto fishing boats and ferries—anything that would float—and sailed out to sea. Ford had ordered US Navy ships into the area, and they plucked thousands out of the water. Thousands of others, however, never made it, perishing in the open ocean. On barges carrying refugees down the coast, many others died of thirst and starvation.

On April 4 an Air Force Galaxy C5-A jet bearing 243 orphaned Vietnamese children and infants crashed into some rice paddies, killing 138 of the orphans. There seemed to be no end to the horror. But there were points of light in the darkness. The next day a second flight transported the surviving children along with many others to San Francisco, where President Ford and the first lady met them.

Once again—as when he ascended to the presidency, offered clemency to draft evaders, and pardoned Nixon—Ford took it upon himself to lead the country away from the past and toward the future. In a speech to the students at Tulane University in New Orleans, he declared that the war in Vietnam was finished "as far as America is concerned. . . . We are saddened, indeed, by events in Indochina, but . . . some seem to feel that if we do not succeed in everything everywhere, then we have succeeded in nothing anywhere."

April 28, after breakfast and the newspapers (with headlines like RED FORCES WITHIN MILE OF SAIGON), the president received his daily briefing from the CIA and met with various assistants and counselors—Rumsfeld and Scowcroft among them. He then motored to the Daughters of the American Revolution Constitution Hall, where he addressed the annual meeting of the US Chamber of Congress. Ford returned to the White House, talked with Kissinger and other advisors, followed by a meeting to discuss federal aid to parochial schools. He ended the afternoon in a quick five-minute photo op with Miss National Teenager of 1974–1975.

The president attended a meeting to discuss energy and the economy then participated in a National Security Council meeting. He had dinner with the first lady then returned to the Oval Office. Just after 10:30 that evening (10:30 in the morning, April 29, in Saigon), Ford ordered the evacuation of all remaining US personnel from the South Vietnamese capital.

In Saigon, the song "White Christmas" was broadcast over the American radio station. It was the prearranged signal indicating that the evacuation was beginning. All nearby airfields had been destroyed by North Vietnamese rockets and artillery shells; the only way out was by helicopter, and for the next twenty hours more than eighty of them cut across the sky. Everyone in Saigon, including the countless refugees who had come here looking for safe haven, knew what the helicopters signified. The Americans were pulling out. A city on edge gave in to panic.

The helicopters, called Jolly Green Giants, picked up evacuees on designated rooftops, flew out to carriers in the South China Sea, unloaded passengers, then returned to Saigon to pick up more. On the ships, men pushed idle helicopters off the deck and into the sea to make room for more evacuees.

At the American embassy, chaos reigned. A crowd seethed outside its gates. Young men outside tried to climb into the compound. US Marines sitting atop the walls used their rifle butts to push them back. Inside the gates those who had been lucky enough to get in sat quietly with their luggage, waiting their turn to go up to the roof. North Vietnamese artillery thundered in the distance.

Some would make it up and out. Others wouldn't. If it had been up to President Ford, every South Vietnamese who wanted out would have been plucked off one of those roofs and taken to safety. But he had served in combat and knew, just as I did, the arbitrary nature of war. At long last in Vietnam, we all had to accept the reality of the situation and of this war. Some friends would be left behind.

Ford didn't get much sleep that night as he monitored the progress of the evacuation. As I did after working late many other nights, I spent the night in the basement of the East Wing—there was a shelter there for the president if he couldn't get out of the White House in an emergency. I never saw it, but I heard there was a tunnel from that basement that could take you over to the Treasury Building.

By the end of the evacuation, those Jolly Green Giants had carried more than five thousand South Vietnamese out of the country. Some were generals carrying attaché cases loaded with gold bars. Others were secretaries in the embassy who had left everything behind but hope.

The iconic image that sticks in my mind is the one that inspired the scene in the play *Miss Saigon*. An American helicopter sits precariously atop a water tower, an improvised ladder leading up to it from the building's roof. An American leans down to help as evacuees crowd the steps, moving upward—a stairway to heaven in the middle of this hell.

There's something inspiring—and at the same time unnerving and sad—about the photograph. It's a picture of desperation, giving you the feeling that it could all fall to pieces at any moment, an American in the middle of it trying to hold everything together. A picture of our involvement in Vietnam—of what we had tried to accomplish and had ultimately lost.

In the pre-dawn hours of the next day, the final American helicopter, filled with marines, rose from the embassy roof and headed out to sea. It left behind a place that no longer existed—South Vietnam.

The adventure was over. But it was not a lost war. It was a lost cause. Millions had died, but you can't take them with you, carry them around like pieces of luggage. They'll weigh you down. You honor the dead. You remember them. You learn from them. But you have to let them go, or you'll never get off the ground. It was time to move on. The 58,000 Americans who had died in Vietnam would, in a sense, stay there forever.

4

All in the Family

Shot in the Dark

Washington is not a town for the faint of heart. If you have a weakness, it will be found and exploited. If you have thin skin, it will be probed and punctured. If you can't stand the heat, you will be driven out of the kitchen.

On April 10, 1975, in the northwestern section of the city, James W. Howe put the business end of a .45 caliber handgun in his mouth and pulled the trigger. A week before, Howe and his wife had visited the Dominican Republic as guests of Tongsun Park, a South Korean businessman and lobbyist. Accepting a free trip to the Caribbean would not have been an issue for 99.9 percent of the American public. The problem for James Howe was that his wife, Nancy, was part of that 0.1 percent. She worked at the White House and accepting any sort of gift or gratuity put her in jeopardy of violating federal ethics laws. The *Washington Post* got wind of the trip, and a reporter was asking questions. White House counsel Phil Buchen was obliged to open an investigation.

Still, I doubt this one revelation drove Howe to suicide. It might have pushed him over the edge, but a person doesn't put a bullet in his brain because of a lapse in ethical judgment. If such were the case, Washington's population would be considerably reduced. I didn't know the man, nor did I know what demons drove him to pull the trigger, but his death, as it turned out, touched me in an unexpected way.

I got a call from Bill Gulley.

"You're going to take Mrs. Ford to the funeral."

Nancy Howe was not only the first lady's personal assistant, but a close friend as well, and Gulley's news gave me pause. Me, accompany the first lady to a funeral? It didn't square with Gulley's previous position. He was the one who had warned me at the start of my tenure at the White House: don't, under any circumstances, step over certain boundaries with regard to the first family. By way of illustration, he told me about a previous military aide to then–vice president Ford whose overly familiar attitude got him a ticket out of the center of the universe and back to Fort Nowhere.

"Bill," I said, "of course I'm going to do whatever you want me to do, but it's sort of contrary to the, uh, advice . . ." I stumbled through a confused moment, which Gulley promptly cleared up:

"Goddammit, *he* wants you to do it."

And that was that. Gulley wasn't the one who wanted me to go, it was the president. In Vladivostok, he had appointed me to bring him the score of the Michigan–Ohio State game. Here in Washington, he chose me to accompany Mrs. Ford to the funeral of her friend's husband. It was in that moment that I realized I had fallen into a favorable situation—but one in which I had to be even more mindful of my position as a military man in the White House. I was determined not to be an aide escorted out the door and into obscurity.

Seeing Red

Richard Vandegeer, a helicopter pilot in the US Air Force, is the last name etched on the wall at the Vietnam War Memorial in Washington. But he wasn't killed in Vietnam. On May 15, 1975, a little over two weeks after he participated in the evacuation of Saigon, his helicopter was shot down over Cambodian waters.

On April 17, the Khmer Rouge—the Cambodian Communists (literally, *the red Cambodians*)—seized the country's capital of Phnom Penh. It was the start of one of the most brutal regimes of the twentieth century. Over the next four years, the Khmer Rouge would institutionalize a program of genocide that would ultimately kill nearly a quarter of Cambodia's population.

At 7:40 in the morning, on May 12, Brent Scowcroft informed the president that several hours earlier, in the Gulf of Siam (now the Gulf of Thailand), a Khmer Rouge navy swift boat had fired across the bow of an American container ship, the SS *Mayaguez*. Khmer Rouge soldiers boarded the ship, and it was ordered to drop anchor at the nearby island of Koh Tang, about sixty nautical miles from the Cambodian mainland.

On the evening of May 14, dressed once again in my spiffy white waistcoat with the gold epaulets, I worked the late shift, standing at ease or moving at a discreet distance from the president, as he hosted a stag dinner in honor of Johannes den Uyl, the prime minister of the Netherlands. Cocktails were mixed in the Red Room. Cold cucumber soup, beef tenderloin, and hazelnut ice cream with chocolate sauce were served in the State Dining Room. Liqueurs and cigars were enjoyed back in the Red Room. A military string ensemble played in the Grand Hall. In between toasts and entrées, the president and his men—Kissinger, Scowcroft, and Rumsfeld among them—slipped out of the party into adjoining rooms to monitor and discuss the situation in the Gulf of Siam.

Ford had ordered the military to retake the *Mayaguez* and rescue its crew. Some six hundred US Marines, an aircraft carrier, a destroyer, eight helicopters, and a number of fighter jets and bombers were set in motion as the martinis were sipped and the beef Wellington sliced.

It was not a clean strike. Very few military operations involving deadly force are. *War* is often just another word for *chaos*. Mistakes were made and men were lost, forty-one killed or missing. But in the end the SS *Mayaguez* and its entire crew were returned to safe harbor. Ford acted decisively. As an old navy man, the sanctity of the high seas was as real and compelling to him as his vows of marriage and his oath of office. The crew of a ship sailing under the American flag had as much right to US government protection as the passengers on a Greyhound bus rolling through Nebraska.

No doubt it was also a calculated move. In the wake of our withdrawal from Vietnam, the action afforded an opportunity to demonstrate that the United States would not back down. It would continue to protect its interests and assert its power wherever and whenever the need arose. We, the country, needed that.

Later that evening, the president changed out of formal wear and into a gray suit—more appropriate for the press conference he held to discuss the ship's rescue. After midnight, as we headed from the West Wing through the colonnade to the residence—I was walking several steps behind him—I noticed he was still wearing the sheer black socks that went with the black tie.

I was moved by the sight—how we put the weight of command, the weight of the world, on a president's shoulders. A president who is, after all, only human, and who doesn't always wear the right socks. I empathized, felt the burden, the awesome responsibility that he must feel. It was in that moment that he hesitated, turning back toward me, and I wondered what deep insight he was about to share.

"Bob," he said, "how did the Bullets do tonight?"

For me that was pure Ford, able to shut it all down—a man who never went to bed without feeling he had done the best he could that day. He would deal with tomorrow with the same confidence. President Ford was great at resting—the man could nap in a nanosecond. His normal routine, if his duties allowed, was to be in bed by 10:00 P.M. and awake at 6:00 the next morning.

The *Mayaguez* incident is considered the last official battle of the Vietnam War. In the words of one official at the Vietnam Embassy in Washington as it closed its doors: "All the past is gone."

A Pool of His Own

Sometimes the president took the advice of his top aides. Other times he didn't. On the same day that the newspaper headlines proclaimed the freeing of the *Mayaguez*, a smaller story in the back pages revealed that Ford had ordered a swimming pool be built on the White House grounds. Just about every one of his advisors urged him to wait. With the rough economy, and folks struggling to make ends meet, it just wouldn't look good. Their argument was, build the pool now, and you'll enjoy it for one year. Build it after the 1976 presidential election and enjoy it for four.

Ford's counterargument went something like this: Number one, the cost would be covered entirely by private donations. Number two, he was the president. And number three, just build the damn pool. Whenever he took that kind of bulldog approach to an issue, the only person who had a chance of changing his mind was his wife, and if she did weigh in on the pool, I'm sure she was all for it. If he'd asked my advice, which he didn't, I would have suggested getting the Russians to do it. They had built him a pretty nice swimming pool in Vladivostok, and it didn't cost us a penny.

As it happened, the Soviets would be very much on the president's mind and agenda that summer of 1975, but before dealing with them he had to do some business with a higher authority.

Bella Vita

Europe was confused. What, many in the European press wanted to know, was that whole Watergate thing about? Nixon, their reasoning went, had been so adept at foreign affairs; why had he been thrown out with the trash? And who was this Ford character, plucked out of the Washington backwaters and enthroned in the White House as the leader of the free world?

At the end of May, Ford made his first trip to the Continent as president, visiting Brussels, Madrid, and Salzburg in Austria, and concluding his journey in Rome. For many Europeans, it felt like a blind date and shotgun marriage all rolled into one. They waited with bated breath and sweaty palms to meet this mystery man who wielded so much power over them. Economically and militarily, America was Europe's first and last line of defense. Thank goodness for Kissinger, they thought out loud; he was a known quality, a realist, and he would preside over this forced marriage.

I joined the presidential party on the morning of June 3, meeting them at the Ciampino Airport in Rome. From there we took a helicopter to the Quirinal Palace, an official residence of the president of the Italian Republic—Giovanni Leone. Living large is a point of pride with the Italians, and Quirinal brought that point home. Built in 1583 on the highest of Rome's seven hills, it is one of the largest palaces in the world—twenty times the size of Ford's official residence, the White House. I wondered if I should leave a trail of breadcrumbs to make sure I didn't lose my way in the place. I might go off to *la toiletta* never to be seen again.

After the president and first lady finished their meet and greet with various Italian officials in the Palace Loggia, they were escorted to their private quarters. Terry O'Donnell and I were standing in the hallway comparing notes, making sure that all our i's were dotted and t's were crossed, when Kissinger came striding up to us. Henry, a man who always walks with a purpose, was in his element—a Roman gladiator with a German accent.

Approaching us, he asked in his brusque manner: "Ver is my room?"

"Oh, Dr. Kissinger," Terry responded, "you've got a beautiful room. It's down this way, around the corner, and it's right next to the president."

Kissinger looked at Terry, then at me, then back at Terry. "How many times must I tell you? It's not important for me to be close to the president. It's important for the president to be close to me." And he walked away.

Henry Kissinger is not only one of the most brilliant people I ever met, he's also one of the funniest, with the sense of humor of a borscht belt comedian. With that comes an ego to match his intellect.

Sometimes I had to pinch myself. Working for the president, chatting with Kissinger, shaking hands with the pope in the Vatican library. Me, Bob Barrett—lapsed Catholic from the South Shore of Long Island—being blessed by the pope. I have proof. Kennerly got the shot. He gave me a print, and I mailed it to my mom. She put it up on her fridge. Too bad Pop didn't live to see it. He would have had a good laugh over it.

One last thing about Italy. They live large and they love their food. It's one place you don't have to order the chicken.

For Ford, the trip was a huge success. Europe liked what it saw and heard. He was not a great speaker in his plodding, Midwestern way, but it was beside the point. The European leaders were hearing him in translation. They didn't care how he spoke, just what he was saying—which was that the partnership between the United States and the countries of western Europe had never been stronger. He came back to America more popular than at any time up until he pardoned Nixon.

Riding that wave, on July 8 he announced his candidacy for the 1976 Republican presidential nomination. He said he wanted to "finish the job."

Ford had seriously considered not running. It was Henry Kissinger who convinced him otherwise.

"The country couldn't withstand it," he argued. "If you don't run, the world will view you as a lame duck for the remainder of your term in office."

Kissinger himself told me about that conversation. The two men had tremendous respect and regard for each other.

The trip to Europe had given Ford a boost, but the omens were not entirely positive. In Vienna, cameras rolling, the president's bum knee gave out and he stumbled down an airline ramp. The fall would have a life of its own, re-created again and again by a young comic named Chevy Chase on a radical new television program that would premier that October. At the time it was called *NBC's Saturday Night*. ABC had its own new show, hosted by Howard Cosell, which they called *Saturday Night Live*. Now we all know which of those two wound up with the name and a run of going on fifty years.

The road to a second term for President Ford would have its share of trips, traps, and pitfalls.

Hooking Up

July 17, 1975. In Washington, the Israeli ambassador met with Secretary of State Kissinger in an ongoing effort to find common ground between Israel and Egypt. In New York, the municipal government announced that nearly fifteen hundred sanitation workers would be laid off—a sign that the city's financial crisis was deepening. But the biggest news of the day did not take place in New York, Washington, or anyplace else on Earth for that matter. It happened in the sky.

About one hundred and forty miles up, in orbit somewhere over France, an American Apollo spacecraft linked up with its Soviet Soyuz counterpart. The two crews shook hands, exchanged gifts, and broke bread. President Ford gave them a call. The video feed, broadcast live around the world, was a little fuzzy. The significance of the event was not. The mission marked the end of the space race between the two superpowers—a costly competition—that had begun two decades earlier with the launching of the Soviet *Sputnik 1*. It also served as a fitting overture to another meeting less than two weeks away—this time not in the air, but firmly on the ground, in Helsinki, Finland.

Seeing the Light

On July 26, I joined Ford and his entourage on Air Force One as he set off on his second trip to Europe as president. This trek would take us to five countries in eight days—West Germany, Poland, Romania, Yugoslavia, and, the focal and high point of the journey, Finland. The president had come to participate in the Conference on Security and Cooperation in Europe, to be held in Finlandia Hall in Helsinki.

The heads of state of thirty-five countries attended the conference, making it the largest summit of world leaders ever held. Pity the poor Helsinkian trying to get to work over the course of those several days; the event created the greatest chaos of motorcades in the history of humankind.

Helsinki is a gorgeous city, a stirring mix of centuries-old and ultra-modern architecture. As it was the middle of summer, it was also a city of nearly eternal light—sixteen hours of daylight, six hours of twilight, with just a few hours of true darkness. Perhaps it was my Scandinavian half, my mother's blood, rising to the occasion, but I found the place exhilarating—the culture, the atmosphere, the long, bright days, and the extraordinary confluence of major post–World War II figures.

Trudeau of Canada, Schmidt of West Germany, Palme of Sweden, d'Estaing of France, Tito of Yugoslavia, and, of course, Brezhnev of the Soviet Union.

On the morning of Ford's first full day in Helsinki, he met with Brezhnev for two hours. Aside from the usual suspects—Kissinger, Scowcroft, and their Soviet counterparts—among those in attendance were Lodal and Viktor Sukhodrev, the Soviet interpreter.

At the end of the meeting, Ford escorted Brezhnev to his motorcade, both stopping at the front door to exchange a few words. Only three people knew what they said: Ford, Brezhnev, and his interpreter Sukhodrev.

Later, at Finlandia Hall, the US delegation was seated directly across from the Soviets. Fascinated, Jan Lodal studied Brezhnev sitting at his small desk scribbling notes. At one point he was surprised to see Sukhodrev push his way through the crowd, walk directly up to the Soviet leader, and hand him a single typewritten sheet of paper. Brezhnev read it, tore it into pieces, and dropped them into his ashtray. When the speeches ended, Lodal watched the Soviet delegation file out of the hall. Brezhnev had left the torn paper behind. Lodal casually walked by the desk and slipped the contents of the ashtray into his pocket.

Back at the US Embassy, Lodal pieced the paper together and translated the Russian into English. It turned out to be a transcript of what Ford and Brezhnev had said that morning in the doorway. As Lodal wrote in the July 2017 issue of the *Atlantic* magazine, this is what the Soviet leader had said to the American president:

I wish to tell you confidentially and completely frankly that we in the Soviet leadership are supporters of your election as president to a new term. And we for our part will do everything we can to make that happen.

Sound like anything you've seen or read about in recent years? Putin wasn't the first and he won't be the last Russian leader to throw his weight behind an American presidential candidate.

As for the business of the conference itself, the Soviet side came away pounding their chests, crowing about what they had achieved in the Helsinki Accords. Its clauses about the inviolability of national borders and respect for territorial integrity appeared to acknowledge and legitimize Soviet domination of Eastern Europe. But the victory proved to be short-lived. It was another section of the Accords that would ultimately leave its mark on history.

The agreement included a commitment to monitor human rights, with the establishment of a group to bring international attention to the violation of those rights. It empowered dissidents in Eastern Europe and in the USSR to speak openly, move freely, and organize actively. Helsinki chiseled the first crack in the Berlin Wall.

It was an open secret at the summit meeting that Brezhnev's health was in decline. He had suffered at least one stroke, and he lacked his usual vigor, moving slowly and deliberately like an old gray battleship. He held on for seven years before dying in 1982. The Soviet Union managed to hold on for nine more before dying in 1991—the same year that the Wall came down.

The West won the Cold War. Helsinki contributed, as did the failing Soviet economy and the sheer weight of history. But sometimes the simplest explanation is the most salient. James Baker, who had been Reagan's secretary of state in the 1980s, later offered his perspective. Speaking at a college in the '90s, he was asked by a graduate student why we won the Cold War.

"Because," he replied, "our German scientists were better than their German scientists."

Wild West

Lynette "Squeaky" Fromme was a member of the Manson family. Charles Manson was a self-appointed preacher of hate and violence whose aim was to create chaos and insurrection. To that end, in the summer of 1969, he orchestrated a series of gruesome murders that terrorized Los Angeles. Fromme, though never implicated in the slaughter, remained an ardent believer in Manson throughout his murder trial. When he was incarcerated at Folsom State Prison, she moved to Sacramento, the capital of California, to be closer to her beloved Charlie.

On September 4, 1975, Air Force One took off from Andrews Air Force Base, bound for Seattle, the president undertaking a two-day, three-city trip to the West Coast. Lee Domina, another military aide to the president, was on assignment with him for that trip. I was the senior military aide of three working for the president and had been tasked with getting plans together for another trip to Vail. The president liked to say, "Winter brings people to Vail, and summer keeps them there."

After Seattle, there would be stops in Portland, Oregon, and Sacramento. The schedule was typical of his domestic travels: meetings with governors, legislators, and businesspeople as well as attending Republican Party fundraisers with an eye to the 1976 election.

On the evening of September 4, the presidential party flew into Sacramento, the last stop before heading home. They checked into the Hotel Senator, which was a short walk from the state capitol building. The next morning, following a breakfast at the Sacramento Community Convention Center hosted by the California Chamber of Commerce, Ford returned to his hotel suite. A little after ten in the morning he set out to meet with Edmund G. Brown, governor of California. It was what should have been a five-minute walk away.

Where presidents go, people are sure to gather, and Sacramento was no different. Several hundred applauded as Ford emerged from the hotel. But one woman—dressed in red as if she wanted to stand out—was not there to cheer him on or to get a glimpse of him. She pushed her way through the crowd and managed to get within two feet of the president. She stopped, drew a Colt .45 semiautomatic handgun from her purse, and pointed it at his chest. Squeaky Fromme, the lady in red, wanted to make a point.

Secret Service agent Larry Buendorf shouted, "Gun!" and stepped between the would-be assassin and Ford. He wrenched Fromme's arm down, forcing the gun out of her hand.

Another agent shouted, "Get down! Let's go!"

In other words, get the president the hell out of there, which they did. Two agents grabbed his suit coat and forced him to bend down, reducing his target size, and hustled him into the capitol building. There, he continued his day as planned, including an address to the California state senate and assembly. The subject of his speech was the rising problem of urban crime.

Outside, the handcuffed Squeaky shouted:

"Don't get excited! It didn't go off."

Then she started repeating, "He is not a public servant. He is not a public servant . . ."

She later claimed that she only wanted to get the president's attention in order to plead with him to protect the California redwoods. She got his attention. She also got life in prison. Fromme was paroled in 2009 and now lives in a small town in Central New York.

On September 18, 1975, two weeks after the Squeaky Fromme incident, the FBI captured Patty Hearst in San Francisco. Nineteen months earlier, the Symbionese Liberation Army (the SLA)—a terrorist organization based in the San Francisco Bay Area—had kidnapped Hearst from her Berkeley apartment, planning to hold her for ransom. Hearst's grandfather was newspaper magnate William Randolph Hearst, and her father was chairman of the Hearst board.

One of the SLA's conditions for her release was that the Hearst family distribute some $400 million in food to California's poor. Patty's father formed an organization called People in Need (PIN) in an attempt to satisfy their demands. But the SLA never released her. Over time Hearst was either brainwashed, radicalized, or both, leading her to participate in a bank robbery and several shootings.

By the time she was arrested, the SLA had disintegrated—its members either dead, in prison, or on the run. But some of the group's ideas had spread like an infection to those who had been close to it. One of the bookkeepers for the PIN program was a forty-five-year-old accountant from West Virginia, Sara Jane Moore.

On September 19, President Ford began his second trip out West that month, with stops in Oklahoma City, Los Angeles, Monterey, and

Palo Alto, wrapping things up in San Francisco. This time around, with numerous social events on the schedule, the first lady came along.

Everywhere Ford went, he loved to press the flesh. In Oklahoma City, the president and first lady went to the Oklahoma State Fair; they toured the livestock area, and he was presented with a cowboy hat. In Los Angeles, they motored to Malibu, where the president met with student leaders at Pepperdine University and then received an honorary law degree to go with his cowboy hat. In Monterey, the president played golf at Pebble Beach. In Palo Alto, he participated in the dedication of the new law school building at Stanford University and met with more student leaders. In San Francisco, the president—unaccompanied by the first lady, who remained on Air Force One, as this was a quick trip in and out of the city—addressed approximately a thousand members of the World Affairs Council of Northern California at the Saint Francis Hotel. Then, returning to his motorcade, he was shot at, twice, by Sara Jane Moore.

Ford's contingent of Secret Service agents had sensed something was off, suggesting—firmly—that the president go directly to his car rather than engaging the crowd. There were some three thousand people outside the hotel, many of them protestors, Sara Jane Moore among them. The day before, the San Francisco police had confiscated her .44-caliber revolver, but the morning of Ford's arrival in the city she managed to buy a .38-caliber handgun. She waited three hours for the president to emerge from his luncheon.

His car was about fifteen yards from the hotel entrance. He had walked ten of them before the first shot went off. It was later determined that the sights of her hastily purchased firearm were about six inches off, and that the bullet missed Ford by several feet. An onlooker, a former marine, saw her raise the revolver again and tackled her, the second shot ricocheting and hitting a nearby cabdriver. By this time the president was on the ground under a pile of Secret Service agents. They hustled him into the car and sped off through the city streets toward the airport.

Things moved so fast that the motorcade reached Air Force One before word of the attempted assassination reached the first lady.

I consider myself an expert on marriage. After all, I've been around that block five times. And of all the marriages I've known and witnessed, I've never seen a healthier one than that of Jerry and Betty Ford. Like any couple, they did have their moments—sharp words and heated discussions. Often as not, the arguments were set off by the first lady's feminism. She was passionate about women's rights. The president, more of a traditionalist, would sometimes wish—out loud—that she would tone down her feminism in public, which only intensified her anger.

These were not arguments he was going to win; Betty was an astute debater. But Ford always had one retort in his back pocket, which he brought out often.

On the day of the Sara Jane Moore incident, once the motorcade arrived at the airport, Ford calmly sat down, picked up his newspaper, and started reading. Betty, with no idea what had happened, asked:

"How did it go?" meaning his speech.

Ford told her his account of the attempted assassination. She reacted as most wives would, with shock and concern.

Ford, still reading the newspaper, drolly said, "Well, all I know, Betty, is that no man has ever tried to shoot me."

Sara Jane Moore apparently had two thoughts going through her head when she took aim at the president. One, that the assassination would trigger a violent revolution in the United States, and two, concern that she would be late picking up her son. The revolution failed to materialize, but, as it turned out, she was late picking up her son. She was also sentenced to life in prison and was paroled in 2007. After that, she vanished into oblivion.

I suspect that if the Secret Service had their way, Air Force One would never touch down in Northern California again. But San Francisco was not the only city that would prove problematic to Ford. The East Coast had its share of issues as well.

Urban Jungle

A Vietnam vet named Travis Bickle, afflicted with insomnia, takes a job as a cabdriver, cruising the streets of New York City by night. It's a world of dark, dangerous shadows and harsh neon light, of decay, filth, and corruption. Drug addicts, teenage prostitutes, and violent pimps roam the garbage-covered sidewalks. Travis captures the zeitgeist: "This city's like an open sewer."

He fantasizes about assassinating a presidential candidate and acquires a small arsenal of handguns. But when that plan goes awry, Travis turns his firepower on a pimp running a twelve-year-old hooker. When the orgy of bloodshed is over, the pimp dead, Travis puts the gun to his own head and pulls the trigger. But he's run out of bullets. The media hails him as a hero for cleaning up the scum and saving the girl. It's as if the war in Southeast Asia had landed in the middle of Manhattan. We had gotten out of Vietnam, but Vietnam just wouldn't get out of us.

The movie *Taxi Driver* was filmed in New York in the summer of 1975, and at the time many Americans, like Travis, viewed the city as "an open sewer." In *my* view, New York gets a bum rap. Sure it has its dark side, but then so do we all. I was born in Brooklyn and have lived in Manhattan, and I've always found the city to be a vibrant, vital place. Contrary to popular belief, ninety-nine out of a hundred New Yorkers are amicable and eager to talk. It's a city of spur-of-the-moment friendships—even with taxi drivers.

In 1975, however, the city was in a particularly tough spot. Everything is amplified in New York, and when the US economy stagnated, the city's economy went into a tailspin. The loss of middle-class taxpayers to the suburbs furthered the hemorrhage.

For years, through creative accounting, the city had been spending more than it had coming in, and now the bills were coming due. Tens of thousands of city workers were laid off. Others went on strike when their wages were frozen. Garbage was indeed piling up in the streets. Rush hour traffic went from a crawl to chaos, as there were no traffic cops to direct it.

Day care and senior centers, as well as hospitals, were shut down. America's biggest—and wealthiest—city was headed for bankruptcy.

For many across the country, and in Washington, New York was simply getting its just deserts. The mayor of New York was Abraham Beame, an accountant by trade and from all appearances a thoughtful, decent man. He wasn't up to the job, however. Not that he was to blame for the financial crisis, but New York City is a big stage, and it calls for a bigger, theatrical personality to run the show—LaGuardia, Lindsey, Koch, and Giuliani all come to mind.

On October 20, Beame went to Congress to plead for billions of dollars in federal loans. Typical of Washington's response, a Kentucky representative said:

"My constituents would be more interested in spending their tax dollars for a new post office in Seattle than in helping New York."

Over the next week, however, a bill slowly took shape in a Senate committee that would provide aid to the city, contingent on additional budget cuts and federal oversight. By October 28, the bill appeared to be headed for approval.

One of President Ford's core beliefs was fiscal responsibility. He had worked his way through high school, college, and law school, never taking a handout; individuals, as well as governments, he thought, must be answerable for their actions. On October 29, the same day that the New York stock market had crashed forty-six years before, Ford dropped the hammer. He said he would veto any bailout of New York City.

The next day, the *New York Daily News* ran the famous, if unfortunate headline: FORD TO CITY: DROP DEAD.

Of course he never said those words. As a future president might say: *Fake news!* But the headline did reflect how many New Yorkers felt—abandoned at sea and sinking fast. How was it that the *Mayaguez* warranted a rescue, but the biggest city in the country did not?

The Bronx is the only part of New York City connected to the mainland. The rest is made up of islands, between thirty-six and forty-two depending on the tides. Financially, however, the city is no island at all. Top bankers worried that if New York defaulted on its loans, markets around the world would collapse.

I rarely disagreed with the president—and it didn't matter a whit if I did—but this was one of those times. Sure, New York had its problems. But not offering the help requested would cause even more for everyone. As an American and a New Yorker, I was entitled to my opinion. As a military aide to the president, I was obliged to keep it to myself. If I had said word one, there would have been hell—and Bill Gulley—to pay.

Over the next few weeks, compromises were reached, and Ford's position softened. He was never an ideologue and was always looking for solutions. New York would not go into default and would not sink into the sea as many might have hoped.

There was another reason for Ford's ambivalence toward New York, and it had nothing to do with the city itself. It had to do with politics. New York was seen as a bastion of liberalism, and he had to tend to the right wing of his party. On November 20, 1975, out on the West Coast, former actor, television star, and governor of California Ronald Reagan made it official: he was challenging Ford for the Republican nomination for president in 1976. And one New Yorker was a casualty of the Republican Right, which loved Reagan so much. That same month Rockefeller announced he would not be Ford's running mate.

The political season was on. And, as it happened, for me, so was the mating season.

Blue Hawaii

It was a big, complicated trip, beginning Saturday morning, November 25, as the president and first lady took off from Andrews Air Force Base for Anchorage, Alaska. After inspecting the Trans-Alaska Pipeline

System—built in response to the oil crisis—and an overnight stay, the presidential party continued to Tokyo. Then, within hours, it was on to Beijing, in the People's Republic of China.

There, over the course of the next five days, the president met with Premier Zhou Enlai and Chairman Mao, continuing the process of normalizing relations with the People's Republic. He also attended a ping-pong match and perfected his chopstick technique with the help of Deputy Prime Minister Deng Xiaopeng, later to become the paramount leader of the country. The trip continued with daylong stops in Indonesia and the Philippines and wrapped up in Hawaii on December 7, the thirty-fourth anniversary of the bombing of Pearl Harbor.

That's where I came in, joining the Fords on the last leg of their journey, in Oahu. I had been on the advance team in Alaska and then had come down to Hawaii to prepare for the president's arrival there. Ford was headed back to Washington that night, but, unexpectedly, Mrs. Ford decided to stay on in Hawaii for a few days. Which meant someone would have to stay behind to coordinate whatever assets she might need—motorcades, communications, Secret Service, etc. That someone was me. An unforeseen three-day layover in Honolulu—not a bad assignment.

Dick Cheney had just recently taken over as President Ford's chief of staff from Donald Rumsfeld, who was named secretary of defense. Within days after assuming his new assignment, Cheney came to me and said that the president wanted me to be responsible for the first lady's calendar of events. For this Hawaii trip, that meant scheduling a visit to a school for children with disabilities and a fundraising cocktail party at her hotel—all a day at the beach compared to the endless complexities of the president's agenda. My title was military aide to the president, with my chief duty of carrying the football. But the job of a president's aide, military or civilian, entails doing whatever the president wants us to do—and my life has been much richer for having done so.

Lady Liberty

Honor's Foxfire Liberty Hume (AKA Liberty) was the Fords' golden retriever—a gift to the president from his daughter, Susan, and photographer David Kennerly. Several weeks after the Fords returned from the Far East, Liberty's vet announced that the retriever was in heat.

The Fords decided to breed her, but for her not just any mate would do. Only the best for Honor's Foxfire Liberty Hume. They shipped her out to a top breeder in Oregon. The problem was the breeding didn't take. She was shipped back to Vail, where the Fords had come for the holidays.

"I'm afraid," Mrs. Ford told me, "Liberty simply lived in sin for a week in Oregon."

The other problem was the Fords had been overly generous in promising puppies to their friends.

"I think," I pointed out, "that Liberty will have to produce a litter of about eighty-four pups."

And here they were with the prospect of zero pups to fulfill the high demand.

Enter John Purcell. And Bart.

A Vail restaurateur who had grown close to the Fords, Purcell has a unique, audacious personality and the ability to get away with the most outrageous things. We hit it off immediately. He had no clearance whatsoever but seemed to have unfettered access to everyone in the Ford administration—including Liberty. When John heard that she had failed to hook up in Oregon, he said, "We can get Bart!"

"Well," the president said, "I don't know about that."

Bart, belonging to Vail native Packy Walker, may have been a purebred golden retriever—he had the papers to prove it—but he was also a bit of a beast. Bart was a beer-guzzling bar dog, hanging out on a stool at John's restaurant, wandering the streets of Vail at will, and carousing all night long. Clearly, he didn't breathe the same rarefied air that Liberty did. But

Purcell can be very convincing. Also, Liberty was on the clock; she'd only be in heat for so long. The Fords acquiesced. Bart was on.

A date was set up, as was a cage in the garage of the Bass residence—the house on Mill Creek Circle where the Fords were staying. Bart arrived, at the appointed hour, accompanied by John Purcell. We all went into the garage, where Liberty was waiting in her gilded cage. John gave voice to Bart's thoughts:

"So let me get this straight. I get to go into the cage with this blond bombshell, you lock it up, and I can have my way with her as long as I like?"

That was the idea. Giving the prospective lovers their privacy, we all headed up to dinner. A couple of hours later, we checked back in to see how the blind date went, and there was Bart—big, strong, macho Bart—sprawled on the floor of the cage. He could barely lift his head. Liberty, meanwhile, was sitting in the corner, licking her paw. Now John gave her voice:

"Really? Is that all you've got?"

Purcell is a man of many talents. I'm pretty sure, for instance, that he's the only person who had never had a background check to fly Air Force One while a sitting president was aboard. Purcell, Kennerly, O'Donnell, me—we were a band of brothers, determined to see how far we could push the envelope. Ford loved it. He was the unindicted co-conspirator in all the pranks we pulled. As president, he knew he couldn't take part, but he could sit back and enjoy his court jesters at work.

As 1976 rolled in, the campaign for the Republican nomination went into hyperdrive. Reagan was gaining ground, tension around the president was building, and we were always looking for creative new ways to break it.

Slick Moves

The early polls were not looking good for Ford. Reagan led among Republicans as well as Independents. The right wing of the party was looking to install a new sheriff in town, and they found their man in the tough-talking guy with the cowboy boots from out West. The race to the Republican nomination was going to require sharp elbows and brass balls.

Reagan took the first shots, accusing the Ford administration of selling out Eastern Europe at Helsinki, of negotiating to surrender the Panama Canal to Panama, and of failing to prevent the fall of South Vietnam. The Ford team fired back: Reagan tended to shoot from the hip and play fast and loose with the facts, and he didn't have the necessary gravitas to occupy the Oval Office. Over the next six months, the rift in the GOP grew wider and deeper.

At the end of January, I accompanied the president on his first campaign trip of the year, to his home turf of Michigan. There, addressing Midwestern Republican leaders, Ford tossed a few darts at the Democrats for attempting to expand the federal bureaucracy at the expense of state and local governments and got off a barb at Reagan as well. Without naming names, he denounced the idea, proposed by his Republican opponent, of privatizing Social Security. Ford relished the challenge—his first presidential campaign.

By February, Reagan had lost some of his luster. He often improvised his answers, a strategy that can work on a local level, but that has bitten many politicians in the ass when dealing with the national press. When asked how he was going to cut the federal budget, Reagan pulled some numbers out of his hat and later had to walk them back. Ad-libbing and backtracking is not a formula for political success. Reagan's candidacy took a hit.

On February 24, Ford eked out a victory in New Hampshire, the country's first primary. Several bigger primaries were coming up—Illinois and Florida among them—and with each campaign event, Ford upped his game. Campaigning for president agreed with him. Meanwhile, Kennerly, O'Donnell, and I took every opportunity on the campaign trail to do our best impression of the Marx brothers—or the Three Stooges. Occasionally, we even managed to enlist Cheney to the cause.

The evening of Friday, March 12, the president gave a speech to an overflow crowd in a high school gymnasium in Buffalo Grove, Illinois, a village outside of Chicago. As I acknowledged before, the president was not a great speaker. He was a Ford, not a Lincoln. He'd get where he wanted to go, but without much flash. What he did have, though, was emotion; he believed in what he said, and it showed. His fervor could be infectious. And after all, this was Ford country, and he had that Midwestern Republican congregation in the palm of his hand. He was no rock star, but in the right place, in front of the right crowd—like in that gym, on that night—President Ford could raise the roof.

The four of us were in the big institutional high school kitchen directly adjacent to the gym, and we could hear every word and every cheer. We felt the thrill going through the crowd. He was giving a hell of a speech, and we knew when he was done, he was going to come back into the kitchen puffed up like a rooster. This was the fourth or fifth event of the day, and we were drained, tired of the campaign routine and desperately in need of amusement. We decided to have a little fun—at the president's expense.

When he had arrived at the school, a group of students had presented him with a stuffed buffalo—their mascot. It would serve our purpose. We sat the shaggy bison down in a spot the president couldn't miss. And then we waited.

"Thank you all very, very much," the president said, wrapping up his speech. He backed out of the gym, waving to the crowd, and we scattered like thirteen-year-olds into our hiding places behind the huge kitchen islands covered with pots and pans.

Ford turned into the kitchen expecting to be met by his entourage. But the only one there to greet him was the buffalo, with a sign tied around its neck: *NICE SPEECH.*

"All right," he said, smiling, "where are you guys?"

He loved it. The president couldn't tell a joke to save his life, but he had a great sense of humor and enjoyed it when we took liberties with him. It made him feel like he was one of the guys, which, of course, he wasn't and couldn't be. But it was a welcome break from the stresses of the office and the campaign, if only for a few minutes. The buffalo had done its job.

Ford won both Illinois and Florida. He was on a winning streak, and the Reagan campaign was running out of money and running out of time. Republican power brokers were calling on him to quit the race in the name of party loyalty. Ford had all the momentum; he was sitting pretty in the Oval Office.

On March 17—just twenty-four hours after his big victory in Illinois—the president welcomed Liam Cosgrave, the prime minister of the Republic of Ireland, to the White House. It was Saint Patrick's Day. That night, a state dinner was held in the prime minister's honor. The president wore black. The first lady wore green. Irish whiskey was served, and toasts were made to the saint who brought Christianity to the island and drove the snakes out of it.

After dinner, Ben Vereen performed, followed by dancing in the Grand Hall. Cheered by his string of primary wins, the president was in a buoyant mood. Big handsome man that he was, Ford liked to turn on the charm at these events and show off his moves on the dance floor. He was receiving attention from the socialite and jewelry designer Princess Virginia von Fürstenberg and beckoned for me to come over.

"Tell the band I'm going to dance," he said, which meant that he wanted something to which they could do the foxtrot. I conveyed the message to the bandleader of the excellent military band for the night and asked for Frank Sinatra's "The Way You Look Tonight."

Unbeknownst to me, a minute later Prime Minister Cosgrave stepped up to make his own request. The president, slick Willy that he was, with the beautiful princess on his arm, stepped out onto the floor, ready to wow her—and the entire room—with his smooth moves. And then the band started to play . . . an Irish jig. Apparently a visiting prime minister outranks an army aide. Again, if looks could kill, I would have been dead on the spot, the president's eyes a firing squad.

Later, I escorted the president and first lady up to the residence for the night. The moment the elevator door closed, he said:

"You know, Bob, if I can't get some decent music around here, I'm going to stop coming to these things."

Betty rolled her eyes. *Good luck with that, Mr. President*, I wanted to say, but bit the inside of my cheek instead.

Voice from Above

Anti-aircraft guns on the roof of the White House are manned twenty-four hours a day. Fighter jets are ready to scramble at a moment's notice. On the ground, every window in the building is bulletproof, and infrared cameras detect any movement outside. Emergency response teams are always in place to, well, respond to emergencies. The White House is a fortress. Along with the Secret Archives of the Vatican and the Federal Reserve Bank in New York, it is one of the most secure, heavily guarded places on Earth.

But not secure enough to prevent one man from breaching its firewall. And not only did I bear witness to the crime, I was a partner to it. One of the invited guests at the Saint Patrick's Day state dinner was John Purcell—the very same John Purcell who had convinced the Fords to allow Bart, the dog, to take liberties with Liberty.

Whenever John was in Washington, the president insisted he stay at the White House, and the morning after the state dinner, John came down to the East Wing to see what I was up to. Not much, apparently. Geniuses that we were, we put our heads together and came to the conclusion that the grid of panels in the East Wing ceiling could easily be dislodged. A ladder was secured, and up John went, crawling onto a beam in search of mischief.

I took the precaution of giving the Secret Service a heads-up, knowing that if they happened upon a foreign body knocking around in the White House walls, John might have lost *his* head in the ensuing chaos. My part in the caper complete, I took up a strategic position in the hallway.

Ex-marine Bill Gulley sat working at a desk just outside Brent Scowcroft's office. He was completely absorbed and fully engaged in his paperwork, a military man from his brush cut to his gray wool socks. Slowly, quietly, a ceiling panel just above and behind him slid forward. John's head and shoulders came into view.

"Whatcha working on?" he asked softly.

Gulley looked up from his work, puzzled. I was the only one around, and I hadn't said a word. I was Mr. Nonchalant.

"Is it classified?" John inquired.

Finally looking up, Gulley—the toughest guy in the building—jumped out of his skin.

"You crazy sonuvabitch!" he yelled.

"Hiya Bill."

John's mother was a tiny woman with a tiny voice. "John," she'd say when she heard about his White House shenanigans, "God is going to punish you." And clearly, if God didn't do it, President Ford saw that no one else would.

Fight or Flight

Saturday, March 20, Ford flew down to North Carolina. Reagan was on the ropes, and the primary there on that coming Tuesday was Ford's chance to knock him down and out. On Sunday, Reagan virtually conceded the primary to the president, saying he would be satisfied by "a close race." A sixth straight loss, however, would have hit him where it hurt most: in his fundraising. Political donors don't throw good money after bad. But the former governor of California had a secret weapon.

Like Reagan, Jesse Helms came to politics through the mediums of radio and television—a conservative commentator and progenitor of today's Fox News personalities. His stances against the civil rights movement, feminism, abortion, and détente with the Soviet Union struck a chord in North Carolina, at least among white North Carolinians, and in 1972, riding the coattails of Nixon's 40 percentage point victory over McGovern, Helms became the first Republican senator in the state since 1903. He threw his support and political machine behind Reagan, who won the primary by 7 points. Reagan had been staggered but was still standing. It was going to be a long bruising fight.

After Ford won two more primaries in northern industrial states, Reagan began his march through the South and Midwest, notching impressive victories in Texas, Georgia, Indiana, and Nebraska. The Reagan campaign's strategy—an outsider running against the Washington establishment—is one that would become more and more common in the coming decades, culminating in the victory of Donald Trump in 2016.

Throughout the spring, the two candidates traded cuts, dividing the Republican pie between them. The question was, could the pie be cobbled back together come November?

The next big test would come on May 25. Six states—at the time the most primaries on a single day—were in play. Reagan had a clear advantage in Arkansas, Idaho, and Nevada and a slight edge in Kentucky and Tennessee. Oregon appeared to be up for grabs. For Reagan, taking all six states would give him the aura of a winner. For Ford, taking at least Oregon would break his opponent's apparent stranglehold on the South and West. As for Purcell and me, the peregrinations of Air Force One gave us the opportunity to take our campaign of comic relief on the road—and across the country.

It wasn't lost on me that as the pressure of the campaign mounted, Ford liked to have me around. On primary nights, he'd often have me up in the residence, joining his family and closest aides, to watch the returns come in. My nonpolitical presence—that I was there neither to offer advice nor to discuss strategy—appeared to be a comfort to him.

On Saturday, May 22, the presidential party flew into Oregon, and I joined them in Portland. Ford attended a campaign rally, gave some interviews to the local press, and the following day, Sunday, he went to church, then gave a speech at a college sponsored by a fundamentalist Christian group. He spoke about the importance of bringing the Bible into our national life. Nothing brings you closer to God than a fatal illness or a political campaign.

The president had invited John Purcell to join him on this western swing, and the night before Ford's Bible speech John and I went out for a few drinks in a Portland bar. I believe we might have broken a commandment or two.

The trouble started with the other guy. I'm not easily provoked, but this fellow managed to do so. He seemed to be determined to get under my skin. He had somehow gotten it into his head that John and I stood between him and the bartender and his next drink. He threw some colorful language our way, but sticks and stones, I just turned my back on him. It was when he grabbed my shoulder to turn me back around that the red light went on in my head, and the idea of tossing him over the bar seemed a good one.

Clearer heads prevailed, and, strangely enough, in this case the clearer head belonged to Purcell. He recognized that military aides to presidents shouldn't be roughing up bar patrons—especially in election years—no matter how justified the roughing up would be. He hustled me out of the bar before I did something stupid that might land me somewhere outside the White House.

The next day, on our flight out of Oregon to El Toro Air Force Base in California, John shared the story of the bar scrap with the president. By the time Purcell was done recalling and embellishing the events of the previous night, I had nearly set off a riot, and he had saved me from an angry, bloodthirsty mob of Oregonians.

"Better be careful, Bob," Ford said.

"I will, Mr. President."

Purcell, satisfied that his work was done, wandered off. I didn't see him again until I strolled up to the cockpit and found him sitting in the copilot's seat, in an oversized Air Force hat that came down over his ears. He looked back at me with a big grin. Surely, the pilot had not turned the controls over to him. I shook my head and turned back around. At 20,000 feet, I figured it was a good thing that Ford had gone to church that morning. Maybe God would save us from Purcell.

"Mr. President, you know Purcell's flying the plane?"

"Okay, Bob."

On the ground at El Toro, passing the cockpit, Ford looked in and said, "Nice landing, John."

On May 25, Ford won in Oregon, Kentucky, and Tennessee. That, too, was a nice landing. Typical of his Boy Scout style, he called the day "Darn good." Damn straight.

5

Ford Tough

Long, Hot Summer

It was clear now that the Republican nomination would not be decided until mid-August, at the convention in Kansas City. But even in the midst of this marathon of a race, there was time to reflect and reason to celebrate.

July 4, 1976. The United States of America was two hundred years old, and it threw itself one hell of a party.

The president's itinerary that day took him first to Valley Forge in Pennsylvania, where the Continental Army under General George Washington had emerged as a disciplined fighting force. From there, Ford traveled to Philadelphia's Independence Hall, where the Declaration of Independence had been signed. And then it was on to the New York Harbor to view a flotilla of tall ships, which had sailed into the city from around the world to wish the United States a happy bicentennial birthday.

The night of July 7, the stars came out—both in the sky and on the ground. It was a gorgeous evening, a brilliant moon shining down on a great white tent in the Rose Garden. Earlier, it had been a different story. Late in the afternoon the skies had opened up—cats and dogs, thunder and lightning, three trees struck and splintered on the White House grounds. Then, on cue, the rain stopped. The clouds parted, the humidity evaporated, and the guests began to arrive. Congressmen and cabinet members—the usual suspects—were among them, but so, too, were Bob Hope; television's Kojak, Telly Savalas; baseball legend Willy Mays; and Hollywood legend Cary Grant.

America loves the British royal family. We may have kicked them out of our house back in 1776, but we've kept them close to our hearts ever since. As bad as they were at governing us, they've done a bang-up job of entertaining us. We sigh at their lavish weddings, gasp at their notorious affairs, sneer at their scandalous divorces, and cry at their tragic deaths. It's Shakespearean soap opera, and we can't get enough of it. And when they cross the pond to pay us a visit, we pull out all the stops—twenty-one-gun salutes, crowds around the White House waving miniature Union Jacks, Bob Hope, Cary Grant, and the best center fielder in the universe all invited to break bread with them in the Rose Garden.

Her Majesty, Queen Elizabeth II, and her consort, His Royal Highness, Prince Philip, Duke of Edinburgh, came to our country to join in the celebration of the United States Bicentennial. The irony of her participation was not lost on the queen. In her speech before the dinner, she reflected on how the great friendship between our two nations had begun with such bad blood and that you ignore the past at your peril.

"History," she said, "is not a fairy tale."

The fairy tale of a state dinner—with its diamond tiaras and tuxedoed violinists playing along the pathways—lasted late into the night. I was struck by the queen's simple humanness. That may sound odd, but on TV and in photographs, she comes across as stiff and formal. But here, in her lemon-yellow gown, she was at ease and in good humor—as much a social animal as the president and first lady. And it was inevitable in this particular fairy tale that President Ford and Queen Elizabeth II would end up on the dance floor. After midnight, they stepped out to bust a move.

Unfortunately, the fairy tale turned out to be a fractured one. In a case of poor timing and bad luck, as the president took Her Majesty in his arms and started spinning her around the floor, the marine band struck up "The Lady Is a Tramp." No one seemed to notice—except, as it turned out, a reporter from the *Washington Post*. Somewhere, Frank Sinatra had a laugh, as I suspect the queen did, as well.

Hail Mary

Lies, libel, and dirty tricks are as much a part of American politics as kissing babies and eating pork chops on a stick at the Iowa State Fair. Martin Van Buren's opponents claimed that he wore women's clothing. Rutherford B. Hayes was compelled to dispute claims that he once shot his own mother. William Taft endured rumors that he believed Jesus of Nazareth to be a common bastard. And they all *won* their elections.

In the run-up to the Republican convention both the Ford and Reagan camps slung their fair share of mud. The accusations were considerably less colorful than in those past elections—no charges of cross-dressing or matricide were made that summer—but allegations of trading jobs for votes and of inflating delegate totals appeared regularly in the headlines. The spin doctors on both sides were hard at work, turning words into weapons pointed at the opposing candidate.

By midsummer, however, the consensus was that Ford was inching his way, delegate by painful delegate, toward the goal line. Then, on Monday, July 26, Reagan threw up a Hail Mary—and it would be four weeks before anybody knew if he had completed the pass.

Reagan announced that he had chosen Richard Schweiker, one of the most liberal members of the Senate—and a Ford delegate from

Pennsylvania—to be his running mate should he win the nomination. It was a complete surprise, especially considering that he had insisted throughout his campaign that he would select a vice presidential candidate with whom he was philosophically compatible. He would, he had claimed, never make a selection in a cynical effort to balance the ticket. Which is exactly what he did, in an attempt to assuage moderate Republicans and perhaps pick up a few delegates in the process.

It was a stroke of tactical brilliance. Or a devastatingly bad mistake. Time would tell. (Spoiler alert: Ford won the nomination.) One Reagan operative said that the announcement about Schweiker demonstrated that Reagan was "not so far right that he's falling over the edge." The problem for Reagan was that while some on the right may not have wanted him to fall off the edge, they *did* want him to live on it. A liberal on the ticket just wouldn't hold water.

Jesse Helms of North Carolina, who had done so much to keep the Reagan candidacy alive, now dropped him like a bad habit. He began a movement to draft James Buckley, conservative senator from New York, to be the Republican nominee for president. Reagan's bold gamble was beginning to look like a bad bet.

In 2008, Republican presidential candidate John McCain made a similar surprising move when he chose Alaska governor Sarah Palin to be his running mate. Trailing Democratic candidate Barack Obama in the polls, McCain's campaign needed a jolt, and Palin provided one—for about five minutes. Her acceptance speech at the convention was rousing—charming, pointed, and funny. For one evening, at least, it appeared that a Republican star had been born. But as the campaign wore on, it soon became clear that she wasn't up to the job. McCain had made an impulsive move that ultimately backfired. Reagan's Schweiker gambit was shaping up the same way.

Within a few days of the announcement, several uncommitted Mississippi delegates announced for Ford—a blow to Reagan, whose ultraconservative credentials should have been lapped up by Deep South Republicans.

But then in came Schweiker, out went Helms, and the Reagan coalition began to fracture.

Even so, Reagan's team wasn't going down without a fight. They countered by claiming Ford delegates were secretly shifting allegiances to Reagan. They also sought to change the conversation, by trying to pressure Ford into announcing—before the convention—who *his* running mate would be. Their argument, I suppose, was that seeing as how Reagan had made the mistake of naming a running mate early, it was only fair that Ford make the same mistake.

Do You Still Want Me?

ON THE OCCASION OF THE VISIT OF
HIS EXCELLENCY URHO KEKKONEN
PRESIDENT OF FINLAND
THE PRESIDENT AND MRS. FORD
REQUEST THE PLEASURE OF THE COMPANY OF
MAJOR ROBERT E. BARRETT
AT DINNER
ON TUESDAY EVENING, AUGUST 3, 1976
AT EIGHT O'CLOCK
BLACK TIE

As army aide to the president, I continued to assemble the assets he required for his travels and to lug around the football when required. At the same time that I carried the president's nuclear codes, I drew ever closer to his nuclear family. I attended the state dinner for the Finnish president not with epaulets and brass buttons, but with black tie and white shirt as a guest of the president. I schmoozed with the Kissingers, race car drivers Al and Bobby Unser, and the White House chief of protocol

Shirley Temple Black. I danced a tango and mugged for the cameras with first daughter Susan and cut a rug with the first lady. Betty could have danced circles around me if she'd chosen to, but she went easy on me, letting me take the lead.

The following Friday, August 6, I accompanied the first family on a quick overnight trip to Camp David. A film crew was there to capture the 98 percent koala side of the president as part of a short documentary to show at the Republican National Convention. The next morning, I was lounging on the living room couch of the Aspen Lodge with Betty and Susan Ford. Kennerly, that scoundrel, captured the moment when Susan, in a mischievous mood, climbed up to sit on my shoulders and muss my hair.

The first lady got a kick out of it. I'm not sure Bill Gulley would have found the image of the first daughter wrapping her legs around a military aide's head so amusing. He had warned me about getting too familiar with the first family, and here I was becoming a part of it, feeling right at home with them. The events of the next four months would have an enormous impact on all our lives. For me, it would be a matter of either four more years in the White House, or . . . what? After just two years, I was so dug in, I couldn't imagine *not* being with the Fords.

At the state dinner for Kekkonen, one of the guests was singer Tony Orlando. Late in the evening, when many in the party were sufficiently tight to loosen things up, Orlando led the crowd in a sing-along of his hit "Tie a Yellow Ribbon Round the Ole Oak Tree." One line of the song struck me as particularly on point:

It's been three long years, do you still want me?

Over the next four months, that was precisely the question President Ford would be asking the American people. But first, he had to come to grips with Reagan and navigate his way through a hornet's nest of a convention.

Bridge of No Return

Ford would have been shocked and appalled had he lived to see the 2016 race for the Republican presidential nomination. Trump's attacks—both personal and political—on his opponents were antithetical to Ford's belief system. *Never speak harshly of another Republican.* That was his motto. In the case of Ronald Reagan, however, Ford's self-restraint was sorely tested, as was Reagan with his similar famous eleventh commandment: *Thou shalt not speak ill of any fellow Republican.*

President Ford believed he had done good work in the White House. Naturally, he expected a dogfight from the Democrats and the Left. That came with the territory. But a challenge from within his own party, accusing him of not being conservative enough, stunned and angered him. He didn't think it was right that he might be shot down by "friendly" fire.

Nancy Reagan made a speech in a tony suburb of Detroit, fanning the flames. She denounced the "new morality" of premarital sex, drug use, and easy access to abortion. She didn't utter the name Betty Ford and didn't have to—the firestorm of the first lady's interview on *60 Minutes* was still producing fallout among conservative Republicans. Drugs, sex, and rock and roll: the Fords had turned the White House into Sodom and Gomorrah. And the money started pouring into the Reagan campaign.

Ironically, the Fords, one of the most loving, well-adjusted families I've ever known, were being cast as weak on family values—by the Reagans, who barely spoke to their own children. The political contest had turned into a family feud, and now, a year after the Safer interview, Sunday, August 15, 1976, the two families headed to the Republican convention to finish the fight. And there would be blood.

Kansas City, Missouri, a.k.a "Cowtown, KC" and "Paris of the Plains," opened its arms to the influx of Republicans, determined to show them—and the news people who followed—a good time. Beer and barbecue ribs were available in abundance as were champagne and caviar, depending on which parties you attended. But no matter where you were, intrigue, insults, and infighting were in the air.

As part of the president's advance team, I had arrived several days before him, checking into the ultramodern Crown Center Hotel, where the first family would be staying. In the outsize lobby, a spectacular waterfall, surrounded by jungle, cascaded down from several stories up—the feature an apt metaphor for the city during those weeks. It *was* a jungle out there.

The principals, Ford and Reagan, had yet to arrive, but the delegates, activists, and political operatives were landing in force, transforming KC from Cowtown into Casablanca. In the parties and parking lots, lobbies and proverbial smoke-filled rooms, pressure was applied, outrage expressed, and deals struck—only to be un-struck when a better deal was offered elsewhere.

The Reagan forces had one objective. Disruption. Chaos was their ally. Publicly, they said they had the numbers to win on the first ballot; privately, they knew they didn't. But if they could just shake loose a few Ford delegates and convince them to abstain, it would prevent him from getting the 1,130 votes he needed to win. The objective was to get the convention to a second ballot. A sitting president's failure to win on the first would paint him as a loser. How could he win in the general election if he couldn't win over his own party? The momentum would swing Reagan's way.

Reagan's people went to work in the Rules and Platform committees, pressing the hot-button issues that many on the Republican Right reacted to viscerally. Abortion. The Equal Rights Amendment. Gun control. The withdrawal from Vietnam. The Panama Canal. Henry Kissinger. Betty Ford. Those would be the albatrosses they attempted to tie around President Ford's neck.

So how divided was the GOP at the convention? At one event, two of the most prominent figures in the Party—Nelson Rockefeller and Jesse Helms—were some twenty feet away from each other, separated only by the buffet table. The interaction between them was as cold as the ice sculpture on that table, each refusing to acknowledge the other's presence in the room. On the floor of the Kemper Arena, where the convention was being held, debates deteriorated into shouting matches, which on occasion turned into fistfights. That was the Republican Party that greeted President Ford in Cowtown.

Wednesday, August 18. *All the President's Men*, starring Robert Redford as Bob Woodward and Dustin Hoffman as Carl Bernstein, was doing big business at the box office, bringing Watergate to the wide screen—a stark, star-studded reminder that the political scandal had never really gone away. Another movie turning heads—including that of its main character—was *The Exorcist*, the story of an innocent young American girl possessed by the devil—and of the extreme measures undertaken to rid her of those demons.

Ford had become America's exorcist, trying to expunge its demons—Vietnam and Watergate among them. Halfway around the world that Wednesday, another demonic drama unfolded, this one all too real.

The *demilitarized zone*, or DMZ, dividing North from South Korea is, in fact, one of the most militarized regions anywhere on Earth. Fighter jets, tanks, missile launchers, submarines, and destroyers, wielded by two fiercely antagonistic armed forces, stand at the ready to blow the DMZ to kingdom come. But none of that high-tech weaponry figured into the action that hot August morning in 1976. The killing that day was as primitive as it was brutal.

At about 10:30 A.M., a United Nations Command work force, accompanied by an unarmed security detail, set out from the south side of the DMZ to prune a poplar tree that was blocking the Command post's view of the Bridge of No Return—a crossing point between the two Koreas. As the trimming began, fifteen North Korean soldiers appeared to observe the operation. After several minutes, the North Korean commander ordered the pruning to stop. The officer in charge of the United Nations security force, who happened to be an American, ignored the command and turned his back. Enraged, the North Korean sent a runner across the bridge, who returned with a truckload of additional soldiers armed with clubs and crowbars.

The North Korean commander carefully took off his wristwatch, wrapped it in a handkerchief, and put it in his pocket. He yelled in Korean, "Kill the US aggressors," then jumped on the American's back, forcing him to the ground, where he was beaten to death with crowbars and axes. A second American officer met the same fate.

The story ran on the front pages of American newspapers the next day, alongside the larger headline that Ford had won the Republican nomination on the first ballot in Kansas City. He had triumphed over the pandemonium—and over Reagan.

In a show of unity, after midnight, early in the morning of August 19, Ford invited his opponent to the podium to speak. The speech was classic Reagan, mesmerizing and emotionally compelling. I'm sure many delegates left the arena shaking their heads, wondering if they had chosen the wrong candidate. But as I saw it, Reagan was the better speaker, Ford the better man.

Within days of his triumph, the president ordered an overwhelming force, backed by B-52 bombers and helicopter gunships, to enter the DMZ and cut down the poplar tree. It was a symbolic response, but to do more would have risked turning a cold war into a hot one. Ford exorcized one more of the country's demons. The North Koreans ultimately expressed regret over the axe murders, and for as long as there was a DMZ the Bridge of No Return would be clearly visible from all angles.

Ticket to Ride

Ford later said that one of the great regrets of his political life was caving to the ultraconservatives in his party and dumping Rockefeller from the ticket in 1976. He valued loyalty, and Nelson had remained steadfast in his commitment to him. Ford considered his own failure to return the favor as an act of cowardice on his part. That reflects one of the harshest realities of politics: it can lead even the bravest of men, on occasion, to betray their own principles in the name of expediency. It's a fine line. To be a successful politician, you must be willing to compromise. But in so doing, you risk compromising yourself.

The die had been cast, however. Rocky was out, and Ford had to pick a running mate. Elliot Richardson, former attorney general and secretary of defense: too liberal. Bill Simon, former secretary of the treasury: too conservative. John Connelly, former Texas governor: too polarizing. Bill Ruckelshaus, former administrator of the Environmental Protection Agency: too untested on the campaign trail. Howard Baker, senator from Tennessee: too impractical; it was clear from the polls that Ford didn't have a shot at winning any of the southern states, so there was no point putting a southerner on the ticket.

Then there was Ronald Reagan. That was a complicated case. It would have been a formidable ticket, but Reagan (Nancy, that is) was too ambitious, too bitter over the loss at the convention, and too entitled to accept anything less than the position of first lady. Ronald Reagan was out. That left one name on the list.

In Italy, in April 1945, one month before the end of the Second World War in Europe, an enemy shell burst, striking a US Army platoon commander. The explosion shattered his left shoulder, fractured a number of vertebrae in his neck and spine, and riddled his body with metal slivers. One side effect of war is the rapid advance of medicine. As more bodies are torn apart, technologies and treatments are created to patch them back together. That platoon commander's life was saved by the newest of the wonder drugs—an experimental dose of the antibiotic streptomycin. The young soldier from Kansas, Robert Dole, survived—as did his acerbic wit and political ambition—but his full recovery took years, leaving him with a withered and useless right arm.

Senator Dole was a solid choice. If Ford had any chance of winning in November, he had to carry the farm states, and Dole, from Kansas, was strong on agriculture. He was also conservative, but not a right-wing nut: he had supported all the civil rights initiatives of the 1960s. And finally, Dole was a fighter. One Republican operative compared Rogers Morton, Ford's campaign manager, to the Kansas senator.

"Rog is a big old Saint Bernard," he said. "Dole is a hungry Doberman pinscher."

The ticket set, Ford and Dole made a last-minute decision on the last night of the convention. They would kick off their campaign in Dole's hometown, Russell, Kansas. And they would do it the next day. Dick Cheney tried to reason with them. With no advance team in place, there would be no crowds, no dignitaries, no marching bands to meet them on the ground. Just television cameras rolling as a sitting president disembarks on an empty tarmac. It wouldn't look good. Cheney told me the president's response to his argument.

"We're going to do it," Ford said, and that was that. The commander in chief had spoken.

Dick stayed up all night, working the phones, sending a team into Kansas ahead of the visit, doing three days' worth of work in a few hours. Air Force One took off from Kansas City at 10:42 in the morning on August 20 and landed a half hour later in Salina, Kansas, where Ford and Dole boarded a helicopter, which after another half hour landed in Russell. The Kansas governor, the state's other senator, and a roaring crowd were waiting.

"You see," the president said, turning to the exhausted Cheney, who told me this story as well, "I told you the crowds would be here."

Two hours later, after visiting Dole's childhood home and meeting his parents, the president took off for Grand Junction, Colorado. Ford, of course, had been right. It was the perfect mix of emotion, patriotism, and affection, and it played well on the evening news. It was a good start to the campaign. But now, after the grueling convention, was time to take a break—a working vacation.

Having come to Vail to prepare for the first family's visit to the presidential vacation residence, I was in Grand Junction to meet the Fords upon their arrival. I was in uniform and on the job, but that didn't stop Susan, and then Betty, from giving me an affectionate hug. They were all relieved, after the fight in Kansas City, to be among friends again.

The convention had put a strain on the entire family—but especially on Betty. She had been worn down, and it showed on her face. The competition between her and Nancy Reagan was far fiercer than that between her husband and Ronald. Even worse, she had aggravated a pinched nerve. The pain was a problem, but the painkillers she took to ward it off would ultimately prove to be an even greater one. For now, she welcomed the respite in Vail.

Seeing me, the president asked, "Everything set?"

"Yes," I said. "We tee off at five."

Gerald Ford worked hard and he played hard. And so began a long weekend of relaxation—swimming, golf, tennis, and dancing the night away at a local disco. But on the other side of that weekend, a hard reality awaited. The latest Gallup poll had the Democratic candidate, Jimmy Carter, ahead of Ford by more than 20 points, 56–33 percent. There was no dancing around those numbers.

Knowing he had to be the aggressor, Ford made the first move. He challenged Carter to meet him in a series of debates. Carter eagerly accepted. It was game on.

There's One Born Again Every Minute

In 1966, Jimmy Carter ran for governor of Georgia and lost. But he drew just enough votes to force a runoff between the top two vote getters. The ultimate victory went to segregationist Lester Maddox. That he might have been partially responsible for Maddox's election as governor devastated Carter. He cast about for answers and found them on a walk in the woods with his sister, a faith healer.

Carter later called their talk a profound religious experience. He emerged from those woods—and from his period of questioning—a new man, born again. The answer he had found was Jesus Christ. Evangelicals claim to have a personal relationship with the son of God, which strikes me as a kind of spiritual name-dropping.

I have no problem with religion as long as you keep it to yourself. But when you try selling me on *your* religion, telling me that you're special and that I can be special too if only I agree to believe what you believe, that's where you lose me. It grates on me. Which is why I don't believe politics should mix with religion. They are two games played on different fields with different rules. Put them together and everybody loses.

Carter was no different than almost any other successful American politician. They all go to church on Sundays and say *God bless America* at the end of every speech. But there was something about Carter—as a candidate, not as a man, which are two very distinct things—that did not appear to be 100 percent genuine. His smile seemed forced, his manner patronizing, his born-again faith opportunistic.

And that would be a key element of the Ford team's strategy. They were convinced that their man was more likable than Carter. But would that be enough to overcome the 20-plus gap in the polls? The race would come down to one man's likability versus the country's raging desire for change.

That week in Vail, as they left the Kansas City convention in the rearview mirror and turned their eyes to the November election, the Ford campaign made its first major mistake. Republican bigwigs from across the country descended on Colorado to help map out a campaign strategy for the next ten weeks. But the real news was who *wasn't* there.

Ronald Reagan.

The man who had been the choice of nearly half of the party was not asked to come to Vail. Did he want to come? Doubtful. But if he had been invited and turned it down, that would have been a black mark on him. If he did come, which would have been the politically savvy thing to do, it would have amounted to an endorsement of Ford. A single telephone call could have changed the entire course of the election. But we'll never know because the call was never made.

Ronald Reagan seemed to be everywhere during the campaign, tirelessly moving around the country in support of Republican candidates. The one name that rarely came up in his travels was Ford. I suspect that that was because another Reagan—Nancy—had tasted defeat but refused to swallow it. Her lingering resentment and bitterness over the loss, her sense of entitlement that the nomination belonged to them, to her and Ronnie, had infected her husband and prevented him from going all in for Ford. To the Reagans, 1976 was history. They were on the road to 1980.

For my part, I was fully invested in the Fords. My first marriage had fallen apart, and I no longer lived in the fancy officer's quarters in Fort Belvoir. I had found a small apartment in Arlington, Virginia, across the bridge from the White House, leased some furniture, moved in, and moved on. Other than that one day back in July, when my wife packed the kids into the station wagon and drove off, I did not experience a moment of regret or despair. The disintegration of my marriage did not even elicit any serious self-examination on my part. That's who I was. And that's who I am. You cannot change the past, so why agonize over it?

In my own way, I, too, had been born again. I just left religion—and Jesus Christ—out of it. My life was in the White House now. I was content to sleep alone in a rented bed. My marriage had ended. Life went on.

Playboy

On September 3, Viking 2 landed on the Martian plain of *Utopia Planitia*, took some pictures of rocks, and sent them back to Earth.

On September 5, an anarchist hurled a banana cream pie into the face of Daniel Patrick Moynihan as he campaigned for the Senate on New York's Lower East Side. The man called him a fascist pig. Moynihan did not press charges.

On September 6, Carter formally opened his campaign by calling Ford a timid, ineffectual president.

On September 8, Ford shot back that a Carter presidency would imperil US defenses.

Sticks and stones.

On September 9, Mao Zedong died. Death doesn't vote Republican or Democrat, doesn't care how rich, famous, or powerful you are, doesn't consider whether you're godless or born again. When your number's up, you're going down. The only difference is, the Maos of the world get nicer coffins.

On September 10, the *New York Times* reported that "paperwork and red tape cost the American economy $40 billion a year, not counting paperclips." A commission was appointed to study the problem. There were no reports on how much paperwork or paper clips the commission generated.

Over the next two weeks, there would be a hijacking in New York, an assassination in Washington, and, as we would all learn—whether we wanted to or not—adultery in a presidential candidate's heart. The hijacking was executed by Croat nationalists looking to bring attention to their cause. The assassination was the work of Chilean agents, who had put a bomb in the car belonging to an enemy of that country's dictator, Augusto Pinochet. The adultery came by way of Jimmy Carter in an interview he gave to Playboy magazine.

"I've looked on a lot of women with lust," he said. "I've committed adultery in my heart many times. . . . God has forgiven me." Except for the *God has forgiven me* part, many of us could say the same thing, and that was Carter's point. He was just like the rest of us, human and subject to human weaknesses, and he wouldn't condemn others for sins he had also committed. He wanted to make it clear that his religion wouldn't leak into his politics.

Still, Carter's revelations were discomfiting. Not presidential. I couldn't imagine Ford making such a confession. The same goes for Eisenhower, Kennedy, Johnson, or Nixon. Sure, some of them had affairs, some even committed serial adultery. The difference was, they didn't *talk* about it.

Now, of course, we don't stop talking about it. First came Bill Clinton, then came Trump. Presidential adultery is no longer contained in the heart, it's smeared all over the White House walls. The cat, as they say, is out of the bag.

Carter's interview with *Playboy* may have been off-putting at the time, but it was also a sign of the times. The seventies were called the "Me Decade" for a reason. *How do I feel? How can I feel better? How can I feel more pleasure? Enough about you, enough about the country, let's talk about me. How do I improve my inner self?*

Such questions would have baffled my father. He'd improve his inner self by downing a couple of beers at the end of the day, and that was that. But that was old school. Times had changed. During the presidential campaign of 1956, one of the books at the top of the *New York Times* nonfiction best-seller list was *Profiles in Courage* by John Kennedy, in which the author explores various acts of bravery and sacrifice. That fall of 1976, the top selling nonfiction title was Gail Sheehy's *Passages*, in which she demonstrates how to turn predictable crises in the adult life into opportunities for personal growth.

After the assassinations of two Kennedys and Martin Luther King, after the riots in Watts, Detroit, and Chicago, after Vietnam and Watergate, Americans turned inward. They just wanted to feel good about themselves. That was the cultural landscape Ford faced in the 1976 presidential campaign. He had probably read *Profiles in Courage* five or six times and probably had no clue what *Passages* was. Had he experienced adultery in his heart? Was he human? Yes. Would he ever talk about it? Not a chance—even if his political life depended on it.

The Sounds of Silence

In 1858, Democratic Illinois senator Stephen Douglas met Republican candidate Abraham Lincoln in a series of seven debates over the course of two months. There were no moderators and no panel of journalists posing questions. Using only their wits and their vocal cords, often forced to shout over enthusiastic hecklers in the crowd, the two men spent hours rebutting each other, reaching an audience of 20,000 over the course of the debates.

By September 23, 1976, when Ford and Carter met in the first of three scheduled debates—this one in Philadelphia, City of Brotherly Love and cheesesteaks—the methodology and math had changed. Reaching an audience of some ninety million Americans, both candidates appeared overly rehearsed and stiff. The most compelling incident that evening came eighty-one minutes into the debate when an electrolytic capacitor—a thingamajig costing about twenty-five cents—blew, and the audio went dead. For twenty-seven minutes, those ninety million viewers witnessed history: two presidential candidates—shifting their weight from side to side, sipping water, shuffling through their notes—rendered speechless.

The next morning, Friday, Ford woke up to some good news. He had gone into that week trailing Carter by 18 points and went out of it behind by 8. He was closing the gap. Apparently, some portion of the electorate was disinclined to contemplate a commander in chief who felt compelled to open up to *Playboy* about the lust in his heart.

Carter's response was predictable. With a comfortable lead, he could afford to be civil. In the early days of the campaign, he had described the president as a "decent, well-intentioned man." But now, no more Mr. Nice Guy. Carter dialed up the rhetoric. His numbers dropping, he said that Ford "stands in the great tradition of Warren Harding, Herbert Hoover, and Richard Nixon." Subtlety and civility were dead, victims of his shrinking lead in the polls.

Ford pressed his advantage. And it was a huge one. He was president, and Carter was not.

Ford's pollsters figured out that when he traveled, his numbers went up in the place he was visiting and went down everywhere else. Consequently, he cut back on his campaign trips, and instead of going out to America, America came to him. The White House, the Oval Office, the Rose Garden—there are no more effective settings for a presidential campaign. When Ford called a press conference, he'd get on the front page of every newspaper the next day.

The media could be Ford's best friend. But it could also be his worst enemy.

The Meaning of Freedom? It's Debatable

Wednesday, October 6, 1976: election day now one month away.

San Francisco, site of one of the two attempts on the president's life, was now the setting for the second debate.

I had flown out to California with Ford two days earlier, on Monday, and he was in a good, positive frame of mind. The race continued to tighten, and this debate would focus on foreign affairs and national defense—the president's wheelhouse. He was respected by leaders around the world, had gone toe-to-toe with the Soviet Union's Brezhnev and the Communists in China, and had earned the praise and friendship of America's allies in Europe—Britain, France, and Germany.

Ford didn't underestimate Jimmy Carter's intelligence—he was a savvy, whip-smart politician—but surely, in the matter of foreign affairs, the governor of Georgia would not measure up to the experience Ford had gained on the ground, in Vladivostok, Moscow, Beijing, and Helsinki. This would be a golden opportunity for Ford to use his accomplishments on the international stage to hammer away at his opponent's lack of practical knowledge. And for the first three-quarters of the debate he did just that, citing chapter and verse—like a lawyer making his case—for all his successes around the world.

Then the wheels came off, the moment when all of us rooting for the president—whether where I stood, just off-stage in the Palace of Arts in San Francisco, or back in the residence of the White House—wished that there would have been another technical glitch, a loss of sound, dead air. But the words were out—Ford had spoken them for all the world to hear.

There is no Soviet domination of Eastern Europe and there never will be under a Ford administration.

Wait. What? Ford's California curse had struck again.

Carter smelled blood. The media smelled a story. Ford's team smelled trouble. They immediately started to spin.

Kissinger put it this way: "The president said the United States did not *accept* the Soviet domination of Eastern Europe."

But, of course, that's not what he said, and that's not what millions of Polish American, Hungarian American, and Romanian American voters heard.

Ford had blundered into a verbal trap, and behind closed doors Cheney, Scowcroft, and Stu Spencer all urged him to clarify his position. But he took pride in his knowledge of foreign affairs, and the pushback brought out the 2 percent grizzly bear in him. Ford was furious and wouldn't budge. He growled that the media was distorting the meaning of what he had said. He had been to Poland, and he had seen with his own eyes that the *spirit* of the Polish people was not dominated by the Soviet Union.

Ford held his ground, as shaky as it was. But he could see the pounding he was taking. His advisors couldn't convince him to walk back his statement, but the political reality was impossible to ignore. After two days of campaigning in California, he finally took his medicine, telling reporters, "Perhaps I could have been more precise in what I said about Soviet domination of Poland. I recognize that in Poland there are Soviet divisions."

It remained to be seen if the political gaffe, and the delay in responding, would cost him. But with Ford's poll numbers stalled several points behind Carter and twelve days to the election, the team decided to change tactics and send the president back on the road and into the air. And, reaching into their bag of tricks, they found a new way to package the president.

Average Joe

Williamsburg, Richmond, Raleigh-Durham, Los Angeles, San Diego, Seattle, Portland, Pittsburgh, Chicago, Atlantic City, Philadelphia, Indianapolis, Cincinnati, Cleveland, Milwaukee, Saint Louis, Houston, back to Philadelphia, Syracuse, Buffalo, Rochester, Long Island, New York City, back to Long Island, Akron, Columbus, Detroit, Grand Rapids, and finally, Washington, DC.

Twenty-eight airports in twelve days. That was Ford's itinerary, and I often either accompanied him or was on the advance team to one of the cities on his schedule. It was a dizzying pace, but it was working. Ford's numbers began to inch up again. One reason: the Republican National Committee hired a batterymate to accompany him on many of his campaign stops—NBC broadcaster and former Major League catcher Joe Garagiola.

The two would sit for half-hour interviews, in which Garagiola would soft-toss questions to the president, who would invariably hit them out of the park. Airtime was purchased in many of the metropolitan areas the president visited to broadcast the sessions. It wasn't exactly Mike Wallace and *60 Minutes*, but it wasn't meant to be. In fact, the interviews were a way to bypass what we now call the mainstream media and to present Ford to the country in the way the campaign wanted him to be seen.

By Monday, November 1, the day before the election, the race had turned into a dead heat. In less than three months, Ford had closed a 20-point gap in the polls. Momentum was on his side. On that last day of the campaign, he came home to Grand Rapids, cast his vote on Tuesday morning, then boarded Air Force One to return to the White House and watch the election results with family and friends.

The president was so confident of victory, he talked to Cheney and others that afternoon about his plans for the next term—how he was going to boost the economy, seek peace in the Middle East, build on America's détente with the Soviet Union.

But it was not to be. As election results started coming in, it was as close as everyone predicted. Joe Garagiola was upstairs in the residence with the president and first lady, watching the returns come in. Exhausted from his two weeks of constant campaigning, Ford went to bed without knowing whether he'd still be president in 1977. I wandered through the halls of the White House, where the president's staff members were scattered, on pins and needles watching their televisions.

I stayed in the White House that night, in the East Wing. One of the military guys—it might have been me—produced a bottle of Scotch, and we sipped it down to nothing. Early in the morning, around two, Ohio—the state that so often tips the balance in presidential elections—fell into Carter's column, and the networks called it.

The morning after, Ford woke to the news that the answer was *no*—he would not still be president in '77. I've been asked several times which was the tensest, most stressful day I experienced during my time in the White House. When I turn the question around and ask what they think the answer would be, people typically guess the day Ford decided to pardon Nixon or the evacuation of Saigon. Neither are right. It was that day after the loss of the election. All that we had fought so hard for, all the hopes raised as the polls tightened, right up to that first Tuesday in November, all went away with the announcement of Carter's victory. The champagne was taken off ice—all that was left were tears in beers.

The president literally had no voice left—he couldn't speak. The first lady read his concession speech for him, congratulating Carter, using the first person as she spoke for the man she loved.

Several advisors told him that the results in several states were razor-thin—close enough to warrant a recount. But unlike many of today's politicians, who think about themselves first and the country second, Ford quickly dismissed the notion. The country was already divided; he wasn't going to deepen the divide by challenging the results of the election.

As I have never lost a presidential election myself, I can't say for sure, but I imagine that it's very hard not to take the ouster personally—not to feel as though your family has kicked you out of your house. After his loss to Bush in 2000, Al Gore lost his way for a time, growing a beard to hide his despair. Hillary Clinton's loss to Trump in 2016 devastated her, leaving her to wander around in the woods wondering where it all went wrong. Aiming so high, one is bound to take a long, hard fall if he—or she—fails to reach the summit.

Ford, being Ford, took no such nosedive. His disappointment was clear, but so was his acceptance of the loss. He considered every day that he had been president as a blessing and an honor.

What exactly was it that stood between Ford and a second term? Watergate's shadow over the Republican Party? The pardon of Nixon? The sight of Americans fleeing from the rooftops of Saigon? Reagan's attack on him from the Right? The general desire across the country for change?

Take your pick. Any or all those reasons may have contributed to his defeat, but years later, Ford reflected on his sluggish response to his gaffe about Eastern Europe in the second debate: "That was too damned late. . . . Delaying was the worst mistake I ever made politically. I don't know why I was so stubborn. I don't know why I was so stupid in this case."

But there was nothing he could do about it now. It was history, and as Queen Elizabeth II so cleverly put it, history is not a fairy tale. Ford let it go. He was ready to move on. And two days after his defeat, Ford asked me to move on with him, as his chief of staff. It was one of the biggest decisions of my life, but it was really no choice at all.

"Bob," he said, "I know the career you can have if you stay in the army. I sign your efficiency reports. You have a real shot at making general if you choose that career path. But if there's a way you would be comfortable with it, you could stay with me."

On December 17, 1976, I formally resigned from the military. I hung up my uniform in the closet and closed the door. It was all over but the crying. No time for that, though. I was about to get very busy.

The Next Chapter

The transfer of power from Ford to Carter went smoothly. Unlike now, with the open hostility between the Republican and Democratic parties, in those days country always came before party. The political transition, however, was not in my purview. I was responsible for the president's personal transition back into civilian life.

He was eager to move on, ready to start the next chapter in his life. And although he might dictate the themes and subject matter of that new chapter, I, in my new position, was the one who would be making it happen. Both Fords were still young and neither of them were retiring types; I would have plenty to keep me busy: arranging security, travel, speaking engagements, etc. But first, before leaving the White House, the question was where to go from here? Where were they going to live?

Florida was an option. But some combination of humidity, hurricanes, and alligators on the golf courses killed the idea. The subject of Michigan came up and was promptly shot down. The sentimental notion of returning home was pushed aside by the memory of harsh, lengthy winters. There was always Colorado, but if they lived in Vail, where would they vacation?

The answer, which was more of a foregone conclusion, was California—Palm Springs. They had good friends there, and the desert would be good for Betty's health—and Jerry's golf game. The Fords were going west, which meant that I was, too.

My life in Washington had begun with a ride on a military helicopter. It ended the same way. Early in the afternoon of January 20, the day Carter was sworn in as president, I joined the former first family as they boarded a helicopter for a ride to Andrews Air Force Base. Ford had just lost an election in which millions of people had voted against him. Far from bitter, however, he had made peace with the people's choice and asked the helicopter pilot to circle around the capital to give us a chance to look down and reflect.

About sixty people were at Andrews to see us off—everyone from cabinet officers to restaurant owners, there to shake his hand and say goodbye. Air Force One took off to fly straight to California. It wasn't long until the small talk and chatter settled into a silence that permeated the plane. There was nothing else to be said.

When we landed, the former president got in a car and went straight to Pebble Beach. He took off the suit he had worn for Carter's inauguration, donned his golfing clothes, and teed off with Arnold Palmer in the Bing Crosby Invitational Pro-Am Golf Tournament. He walked the rope line, shaking every single person's hand.

"Thank you, thank you," he said thousands of times.

Ford played three rounds with his good friend Arnie that Thursday, Friday, and Saturday. Yes, a new chapter had begun.

It had been a good run, life-changing for me, but I, too, was ready for the next chapter. Various presidents and former presidents, moguls, millionaires, and movie stars—along with a parade of wives and other women—would have a page in my life. But none would play a more inspiring role than Betty Ford. She was neither a wife nor a girlfriend, but she was family.

I've said before that I've never met anyone tougher than Betty. But the White House had taken its toll on her, and several months after the ride out of Washington, I would discover just how breakable she was.

6

A Politician's Wife

I once asked Betty Ford what the saddest day of her life was, expecting her to say it was the day she lost her father. But she surprised me, responding without hesitation: *August 9, 1974*. The day her husband became president. She hadn't lost a father that day. She lost herself.

By all accounts, including her own, Elizabeth Anne Bloomer had an enchanted childhood. Born in Chicago and raised in Grand Rapids, Michigan, she loved to dance, play football with the boys, and socialize with her friends. They all called her Betty. Not even the Great Depression, with all the hardships it brought into her home, dampened her joie de vivre. To help her family out, she began to earn a little money teaching kids how to dance—which only made her happier. But her enchantment, as well as her childhood, came to a sudden, agonizing end, at age sixteen, in July 1934. Her father died in the garage of carbon monoxide poisoning.

His death was ruled accidental. It was only later that Betty realized that her underemployed, alcoholic father likely committed suicide, thinking, like George Bailey in the movie *It's a Wonderful Life*, that he was worth more dead than alive. Thanks to the official cause of death, his life insurance policy paid out, helping the Bloomers weather the Depression.

Nearly fifty years later, Betty would come close to following in her father's wake, killing herself not in a gas-filled garage, but in a fog of pills and alcohol.

As a teenager, on a lark, she and a couple of girlfriends had gone to a psychic to get a sneak peek into their futures. The two other girls got boilerplate: husbands, families, a nice white picket fence. But when it was Betty's turn, the psychic looked into her eyes and saw something else: "You will walk with kings and queens."

Betty Ford took to the role of first lady with relish, and at times she loved it—the socializing, the chance to express her views, and yes, the mingling with kings and queens. But she had been at Jerry's side in Washington for over two decades, and as much as she loved him—and he loved her—being a politician's wife took a toll on her.

She had once studied dance under Martha Graham and had a dream—a realistic one—of having a successful career as a dancer on the New York stage. But instead of becoming a star, she became the wife of one. While Congressman Ford rose to prominence, Betty did what congressmen's wives were expected to do: attend luncheons, chauffeur and entertain constituents visiting from Michigan. Then, at night, her role would change to mom and wrangler, with four kids to corral. Like millions of others with long days and hectic schedules, at the end of the evening she'd mix a cocktail or two to help her decompress.

Then came a pinched nerve and bouts of osteoarthritis. Her doctors prescribed Darvon to control the pain and Valium to control her anxiety. No one thought twice about it. Half of America was on drugs—to wake up, go to sleep, lose weight . . . ease the pain.

On that day, August 9, 1974, when he assumed the presidency, Ford declared "our long national nightmare is over." In a sense, without anyone knowing it, least of all her, Betty's had just begun.

Tower of Strength

Betty Ford was one of the most independent-minded, outspoken, and admired first ladies in history. Following her famous (some would say *infamous*) *60 Minutes* interview in the summer of 1975, in which she spoke in favor of abortion and the ERA and recognized the possibility that her children had smoked marijuana and had premarital sex, Rumsfeld and Cheney went to the president and said that she had to tone it down. Ford paused for a moment, nodding his head.

"Fine," he said. "*You* tell her."

The big tough All-American from the University of Michigan knew how strong she was. The future secretary of defense and vice president decided better of it. Discretion is the better part of valor.

Betty's willfulness served her well as first lady and as a public figure. But on a personal level, it also did damage. She refused to acknowledge the possibility of a growing dependency on—and abuse of—pills and alcohol. She faced the same burdens as the president—the Nixon pardon, the ugly withdrawal from Vietnam, the two assassination attempts, the political brawl with the Reagans. But her husband had that uncanny ability to leave the past behind him, to shake off the dirt and move on to the next challenge. Betty did not.

The world weighed on her, the emotional stresses of raising a family and running the East Wing exacerbating the pain in her neck, her back, and her bones. To cope, she medicated.

By the presidential campaign of 1976—first against Reagan, then against Carter—small cracks began to appear in her facade. A late arrival at an event. A slurred speech. A missed appearance due to "a twenty-four-hour flu" or "exhaustion." But she soldiered on, even reading her husband's concession speech on the day after the election because he was too hoarse to do it. She was a tower of strength . . . about to crumble and fall.

Rancho Mirage

Norman Brokaw was one of the most powerful figures in Hollywood, an agent at William Morris who had represented, at various times, Marilyn Monroe, Clint Eastwood, and Warren Beatty, among others. Hollywood agents don't have the best of reputations, but in my experience, Norman was a stand-up guy. I think the opportunity to add a former US president to his Mount Rushmore collection of clients brought out his greatest angels.

I was fielding potential deals from Norman before Ford had even left the White House—deals I had to stick in my back pocket until January 20, as there could not even be the appearance that the president was making decisions based on future financial considerations. Once Ford was out of office, however, the dog—meaning Norman—would have his day, bringing with him an assortment of lucrative book contracts, television deals, and speaking engagements.

We had hardly unpacked our bags, and already I was planning Ford's coming itineraries. That first year, 1977, between speaking engagements, Republican Party fundraisers, meetings, and golf tournaments, Ford and I were on the road twenty days out of every month—which were twenty days out of every month that Betty Ford sat alone in her gilded cage at Rancho Mirage, staring out the window at a desert that had become her desert island.

For decades, she had lived in Washington, at the center of American political life, with all its social activities and demands. Then, for two years in the White House, Betty had resided at the center of the world. By an act of will, she presented a sober face to that world, hiding and diverting attention from her escalating toxic dependencies. But now, three thousand miles away and out of the public eye, she had no more reason to maintain even the appearance of sobriety. She let herself go.

Nutcracker

The children of alcoholics are often the first to diagnose the problem—and the first to go into denial. They know the mood swings and they adapt to them. They recognize the self-destructive behavior, and they rationalize it. Even as they grow older, they learn to avoid rather than confront the issue. They've been stung too many times before to poke the hive again.

For years, Betty's children had made excuses for their mother. Driven by a sense of helplessness, they looked the other way. And in a way, all of us close to Betty had become her children—looking but not seeing, adapting, and adjusting to her behavior. I did not have the qualifications, nor was it my place, to confront her. I was no longer military, but I carried the idea of a chain of command into civilian life, and I did not have the standing to stand up to the former first lady.

Norman Brokaw had negotiated a deal for Betty—as well as for her husband—to do commentary for NBC. In September 1977, as part of that deal, she was scheduled to travel to Moscow to narrate the Bolshoi Ballet's performance of *The Nutcracker*. The program would be taped and then aired over the holidays in the United States. It seemed to be a perfect project for the former dancer. But it proved far from ideal.

The president asked me to accompany Betty to Moscow, and we stayed at the historic Hotel Sovietsky. Built at Stalin's behest in 1952, in the "Soviet Empire Style," it was a four-star hotel with a one-star Soviet-style heating system. The Moscow autumn chill made itself right at home in the Sovietsky, and Betty spent her time at the hotel on the bed wrapped in blankets, shawls, and her mink coat. Between the cold and her anxiety over her upcoming narration, she later admitted that she began to secretly pop pills to get herself through the experience.

Not surprisingly, the self-medicating proved self-defeating. She could barely make it through the rehearsals without fumbling over her lines. It was finally decided that huge cue cards would be written for her to read as the ballet unfolded. It was painful to watch. She was beginning to crack. But to me, she remained as endearing as ever.

Moscow has its diversions, and I am eternally grateful to Betty for bringing an excellent one to my attention. On the way to the Bolshoi Theatre the night of the performance, I sat on a jump seat in the limo facing her and the interpreter assigned to her by the Soviets—a lovely young woman named Katryina. Betty's words might have been slightly slurred, but she remained as clever as ever and a sharp judge of character.

"Well, Katryina," she said, turning toward the interpreter, "has Bob been behaving himself?"

Katryina looked me straight in the eyes and said, "Unfortunately, yes."

I had no need of a translator. Her message was loud and clear. My last night in Moscow was going to be unexpectedly entertaining—and the best part would come after the ballet was over and I had gotten the former first lady back to her hotel room.

It's likely Katryina was a KGB agent. At the very least, she would be debriefed after she had debriefed me. But who cares? As I said, I was no longer military, I no longer carried the football, and I had no state secrets to share. Sleeping with the enemy was not a punishable offense; it was the natural conclusion to a wonderful evening. The most she might squeeze out of me was the former president's next tee time.

If the Soviets saw me as a useful idiot, I turned out to be a very useless one. And if Katryina was a honey trap, she turned out to be quite a sweet one. Looking back, I prefer to think that it was simply a matter of human chemistry as opposed to some pointless minor gambit in a Cold War chess game.

For me, the real moral of the story is that Betty Ford, under the influence, was far more intelligent and observant than most people I've known when they are stone-cold sober. Still, I knew that something had to be done. I just didn't know what. It would require a heroic act by someone far closer to Betty than I ever was.

Sowing the Wind

The more things changed . . .

Ford didn't stop moving, and so neither did I. It was as if the presidential campaign had never ended. I returned to Rancho Mirage from Moscow, dropped Betty off, picked Jerry up, and we were off to the next airport, hotel, fundraiser, or speaking engagement. But wherever we were, one thing remained a constant. Every morning, whether we were on a plane bound for our next destination or in his room having coffee and English muffins, the first thing on Ford's menu was the news, a stack of papers at his side, the *New York Times* and *Washington Post* on top of the pile.

Anything out of Washington—stories about tax or energy policy, the economy, or international affairs—he naturally ate that up. He kept up with President Carter, disagreeing with his policies and politics, but expressing sympathy, knowing the pressure that he was under. Ford was careful in his speeches never to directly criticize the sitting president.

But Washington was not the world, and when it came to the news, Ford was an omnivore. If it was fit to print, he was fit to read it—and share it with me. That fall of 1977, as we bounced around the country, Ford became my Walter Cronkite.

Another plane hijacked by Palestinians. Floods in the South, strikes in coal country, racial strife in South Africa, arson in Boston. Ford kept me up to speed on the news back in New York: Son of Sam was found competent to stand trial for six murders, Ed Koch won the race for mayor, and Yankee Reggie Jackson hit three home runs to win the World Series. Another story that caught his eye was that the universe was not going to expand forever but, several scientists theorized, would sooner or later collapse upon itself. Ford told me not to worry. He quoted scripture.

You'll hear of wars and rumors of wars: be not troubled, for all these things must come to pass, but the end is not yet.

I noted that I was relieved to have time to atone for my sins. Ford nodded his head: "And maybe commit a few more, Bob?"

Maybe.

One news item in particular, in the middle of November, captivated Ford—brought out the statesman in him. He literally sat on the edge of his seat reading it. President Anwar Sadat of Egypt was seeking an invitation to speak to the Israeli parliament. He was going to journey into the belly of the beast. By visiting the enemy, Ford said, Sadat will make more enemies.

In visiting Jerusalem, Sadat stirred up new hopes for peace, but he also stirred up some vipers. Two months later, February 1978, in Cyprus, two Palestinian terrorists assassinated the editor in chief of Egypt's most important newspaper—a friend of Sadat's who had traveled with him to Israel. A month later, in March, thirteen Palestinians landed a boat on an Israeli beach, hijacked a bus, and murdered thirty-eight men, women, and children.

Three days later, in retaliation, Israel invaded Lebanon, killing over a thousand civilians in the process. The path to peace was a bloody one.

But the end is not yet . . .

What We Do for Love

As a child of the Great Depression, a guy who needed several jobs and a football scholarship to get through college, Ford was a cautious man when it came to money—specifically when spending it. He was a man who was not ashamed of pinching his pennies.

At one of our many stops that fall, it was in Pittsburgh I believe, we were joined for lunch at a diner by a local Republican councilman. He ate, made his pitch for support in an upcoming election, shook Ford's hand, and walked away, not even offering to pay his share of the bill. Ford was flabbergasted and talked about the slight all the way back to our hotel—getting all worked up over the cost of a hamburger and a Coke, maybe $3.80 plus tip.

Finally, I said, "Have I ever asked you for a souvenir?"

"No," he said, wondering what that had to do with the lunch tab.

"Have I ever asked you for an autograph?"

"No, you never have."

"Well," I said, "I finally want something."

"So what is it?"

"I want the first nickel you ever made." I reached over into his pocket. "And I know it's right in here."

"Well, you!" he said. "There's no reason in the world that I should have paid for that man's lunch."

On the night of March 31, 1978, just before midnight, I had no choice but to go into his room, wake him out of a deep sleep, and take $10,000 out of his pocket and throw it out the window. And he didn't raise a single objection.

We were in Rochester, New York, the first stop of three on this particular trip. Ford was scheduled to make a speech in Maryland the next day, where he would have received a $10,000 honorarium—chicken feed compared to what today's ex-presidents command on the open market; nevertheless, it would have gone a long way to soothing the pain over that burger and Coke.

I had gotten the call at about ten that night. It was Ford's daughter, Susan. She was desperate, frantic even. "Mom's going to die if we don't do something. We're going to do this intervention thing with her. You've *got* to get him home."

No was clearly not an option. Susan was the perfect blend of her mother and her father: tough, beautiful, and smart.

"Okay," I said to myself, "the first thing I have to do is find someone to fill in at the event down in Maryland."

Kissinger. I knew he was down in Texas taking part in some to-do put on by Ed Haggar, chairman of Haggar Clothing, famed for its slacks. I got ahold of Henry, and he said, "Sure, I'll do it, but it's eleven at night, I'm down here in Dallas. How am I supposed to get—"

"Okay," I said, cutting him off. I didn't have time to be diplomatic with the most famous diplomat in the world. "I'll get back to you."

So I called Ed Haggar. Without going into too much detail, saying only that Mrs. Ford wasn't feeling well, I explained my predicament.

"Stop," he said, with a drawl as big as Texas. "Don't you worry about a thing. I'll take care of Dr. Kissinger. You get your man back to the desert to take care of his wife."

Haggar flew Kissinger to Maryland in his private jet. There were so many people who loved the Fords and would do anything for them, because they knew the Fords would do anything for them.

With everything in place, the gears already turning, that's when I went in and woke Ford up.

"Mr. President, we're going home."

At nine the next morning, California time, we were in his office at Rancho Mirage, preparing to ambush his wife. And that's exactly what it was. Poor, petite Betty Ford had no idea what was about to hit her.

There were twelve of us in all, not quite a platoon but larger than a squad, gathered in that office. We had flown or driven in from across the country over the last twenty-four hours, and now we were all going over our notes, quietly, like soldiers checking their weapons before storming the castle.

Susan had traveled the shortest distance geographically, living in the desert nearby, but had come the furthest emotionally, having watched her mother deteriorate by the day. Navy captain and psychiatrist Dr. Joseph Pursch ran the Alcohol Rehabilitation Service at the Navy's Long Beach Regional Medical Center. He had sobered up some of the toughest birds in the world—drunken sailors—and had sent them back out to sea. Now he'd try to do the same for Betty—the intervention was his show.

Also present were Dr. Joseph Cruse, Betty and Susan's personal physician and a recovering alcoholic who Susan had first approached about her mom; a nurse and Betty's personal assistant; the Ford sons, Mike, Jack, and Steve; Mike's wife, Gayle; the former president and myself; and last but certainly not least Clara Powell, the family's former housekeeper who, during several of the busiest Washington years, had become more than occasionally a surrogate mother to the four Ford children.

Dr. Pursch gave us our marching orders: there would be resentment, anger, and crying on Betty's part, but we had to stand firm and be brutally honest with her. Her survival might depend on it. Pain was part of the process of healing. As we stepped out of the air-conditioned office into the glare of the morning sun, burning off the desert night chill, I thought to myself this might be the hardest walk I had ever taken.

Betty's initial surprise and delight at seeing her sons on her doorstep gave way to apprehension as the rest of us trooped in and she saw the somber expressions on our faces. This was not a happy occasion. Her husband took her hand, led her into the sunken living room, and sat beside her on the couch. We all followed, some deploying into the stuffed and wicker chairs set around a coffee table. I stood off to the side, trying to control my emotions. Which we all were—with little success.

Betty wore the same pastel pink bathrobe—a remnant of brighter times—that she wore whenever at home, which was most of the time these days. She looked small and frail, like a doll, lost in the cushions, confusion written all over her face. Jerry put his arm around her.

"We're doing this because we love you," he repeated several times. Then he said, "Mike, you start."

Betty's oldest son began by saying he understood the pressures she had been under as the wife of a successful Washington politician and as the mother of four children. But her chemical dependency was destroying her relationship with their dad, with the children, and with her friends. She had too much to lose. "Your life is too valuable to let it go."

Mike's wife, Gayle, went next, turning up the heat. "Mom, you're always asking when Mike and I are going to have children. We feel very strongly that we don't want to have a child until we know for sure that you are sober enough to be aware that you *have* a grandchild."

I was stunned by the directness of Gayle's comments, but it was too much for Betty. Resentment, rage, then tears filled her eyes. She wanted to speak, stand up for herself, but Dr. Pursch quieted her.

"Betty, please, just listen."

She seemed even smaller now, shrinking away before our eyes.

Jack talked about how, as a teenager, he was always fearful and embarrassed to bring friends home. And now, as an adult, he recalled driving down to see her and not even being sure when he left that she knew he had been there.

"Betty, we love you," Jerry interjected, trying to soothe the pain—but the words only seemed to sharpen it. The former president was powerless.

Steve remembered all the times he had visited her, thinking she might be lonely, only to have one-sided conversations as she drifted off. He would quietly and sadly leave, driving back home.

Now Betty was shaking, as if being shaken awake from those lost conversations with her son. Susan, the only daughter and youngest child, was shaking, too. She had made the phone calls. She had brought the family together. She had orchestrated this intervention. But now, she could only sob, words failing her. She buried her face on Clara's shoulder, just as she had done so many times as a child. Finally, Susan found her voice.

"Mom, when I was little, and even as I grew up, I always admired you for being a dancer. I wanted to be just like you. But now, these days, you're falling and clumsy. You're not the same person. And I've talked to you about things—things that were important to me, and the next day you didn't even remember."

The four Ford kids and Gayle had started something extraordinary—a journey that would save not only their mother's life but the lives of hundreds of others.

Sometimes, when a thing is cracked—a mirror, a bone, a person—you have to break it before you can fix it. On that day, Betty Ford was broken.

Three weeks later, on April 21, I emerged from the Alcohol Rehabilitation Service at the Navy's Long Beach Regional Medical Center—no fancy spa in Malibu—where Betty was staying, rooming with three other women. I spoke to the approximately one hundred reporters gathered there:

"Here is the statement from Mrs. Ford. 'I have found I am not only addicted to the medication I have been taking for my arthritis, but also to alcohol. . . . I expect this treatment and fellowship to be a solution for my problems, and I embrace it not only for me but all the many others who are here to participate.'"

One reporter asked whether Mrs. Ford would be speaking publicly.

"We've never had too much success in keeping Mrs. Ford's mouth shut," I answered. "Somewhere along the line, she'll be saying what she wants to when she wants to."

Her recovery would be long and hard, but most importantly it had begun. The Betty Ford we all knew and loved was pulling herself out of the bottle.

Piece of Work

The Fords' new home in Rancho Mirage, built on the thirteenth hole of the Thunderbird Golf Course, was completed that year, 1978. Designed by the same architect who had created several Los Angeles landmarks, including the Capitol Records Building, it was a modest single-story ranch-style house with a cream exterior and lime-green drapes and couches inside.

It was here that Betty faced her family's intervention, and it was to here that I drove her home after a monthlong stay in the Naval Hospital. We pulled into the short curved driveway, and I came around to open the door for her. It was as though this were the first time she had seen the place—certainly the first time sober. She paused for a moment, focusing on the front lawn.

Since leaving the White House, her husband had taken an interest in contemporary art—the sharp angles and soft curves, the abstract shapes, appealed to both his eye and his imagination. The builder of the Ford house had consequently commissioned minimalist New York sculptor Paul von Ringelheim to create a unique artwork that would greet all comers. Titled *Endless Force*, it was a twelve-and-a-half-foot leaning tower of glittering stainless steel.

Von Ringelheim described it as "an optimistic sculpture with a sense of boundless energy and great vitality. That's the way I see America and the former president's vision of it."

The former first lady described the piece differently. She looked at it, then at me, and said:

"Jerry's last erection."

She turned and went into the house. If I had not been a man of extraordinary gravitas and self-control, I would have lost it right there.

Betty Ford was back.

Our Daily Bread

As a kid back on Long Island, many of my happiest days were spent out on a dusty, worn-down patch of land turned into a driving range, making a few dollars a day retrieving golf balls. Now, for a few weeks each summer, I rubbed elbows with golf royalty, made conversation with Jack Nicklaus, and played rounds with Clint Eastwood, basketball legend Dr. J, and Bill Murray. This was a bigger thrill to me than meeting the pope.

Organizing and being a part of the annual Jerry Ford Invitational golf tournament in Vail remains one of the most gratifying—and singular—accomplishments of my life. Finding players was a snap. All I had to do was mention the former president's name and Hollywood celebrities along with top pro golfers lined up to tee off. And it was all for a good cause. Over the course of twenty years, the tournament made hundreds of thousands of dollars for Vail charities.

It wasn't all about altruism, however. These guys were extremely competitive. Hollywood A-listers and big-time athletes tend to have great confidence in their abilities, putting money where their mouths are. Sometimes golf seemed secondary to the side bets being made, fistfuls of cash exchanging hands at these tournaments. June 1978, the second year of the Invitational, I took a gamble of my own. I took the plunge—and got married for the second time.

Movie stars and golf greats gathered in the late afternoon sun on the lawn adjacent to the eighteenth green at Vail Country Club. The former president gave the bride away. Betty Ford and Delores Hope—Bob's wife—served as bridesmaids. As the ceremony drew to a close, Gordon MacRae, star of the film versions of two Rodgers and Hammerstein musicals, *Oklahoma* and *Carousel*, appeared unprompted on the balcony overlooking the lawn and sang the Lord's Prayer.

Our Father who art in heaven, hallowed be thy name. Thy kingdom come. Thy will be done, on Earth as it is in heaven. Give us this day our daily bread; and forgive us our trespasses, as we forgive those who trespass against us; and lead us not into temptation, but deliver us from evil.

If there is a voice of God, I heard it that day in the clear Rocky Mountain air. For a few minutes, looking out over the eighteenth green, I had religion.

It was a glorious moment. But my best man was there to bring me back down to Earth. John Purcell: you remember him, the guy crawling around in the White House ceiling and later taking the wheel of Air Force One. I told him before the ceremony: *Don't screw this up.* And when the reverend asked me *Do you have the ring?* I glanced warily over at John. He gave me this look, like *what?* I was at a loss. I couldn't very well strangle him in front of the president and the gathered luminaries. John let me dangle for a moment, then tapped me on the shoulder and spit the ring into his hand. Purcell had had his moment, and now the show could go on.

I had been brought down to Earth, but Phoebe, my second wife, hadn't. She looked radiant, and I thought to myself, *This is the happiest day of my life. I've finally found the one.* Five times I've had that same thought, and five times I've believed it with all my heart. I am an ardent devotee of the institution of marriage. Two people building a life together is a fundamental aspect of our species and the foundation of society. I'm not saying marriage is for everyone, but family is the glue that keeps everything from falling apart.

Sex. Love. Marriage. Three distinct conditions. Ideally, they all come together in a neat little package with a bow on it. But we don't live in an ideal world. Putting all three together is something we aspire to and sometimes achieve. I have achieved it—five times.

It was during that June in Vail, between the golf tournament and my second wedding, that I saw a successful marriage in action. The Fords. On the night of my wedding to Phoebe, I was standing in the country club bar talking to the former president. The fellow working behind the bar offered to mix him a cocktail, reaching for a martini glass. But Ford put up his hand and shook his head.

"You know, Bob. I've been thinking about this for a while, and I've decided—in a marriage one person drinking and the other not drinking—it just doesn't work." He took the empty glass on the bar and turned it over, and after forty years of two martinis every night, from that day on, he never turned the glass back up. He stopped cold. He stopped for love.

Turning that glass over, quitting drinking, was one thing. Turning away from the White House, quitting his pursuit of the presidency, was another thing altogether. Power is addictive, and Ford wasn't ready to walk away from it yet. That summer and fall we traveled to hundreds of cities, where he campaigned for Republicans running for office in the 1978 midterms. Large enthusiastic crowds greeted him wherever we went. The polls showed him leading the field among potential Republican presidential candidates in 1980 and put him ahead of Carter in a potential rematch.

The *New York Times* called me for comment. I said Ford had made no decisions about 1980 yet, but (and this was a big *but*) I went on, "He's not going to run away from any responsibilities. He would love to see a young man that can capture the imagination of the party and the nomination, but that's not necessarily developing right now." The official line, in other words, was that he was the best man for the job and remained open to an encore in the Oval Office.

The unofficial line, however, came from another spokesperson—someone closer to the heart of the matter and freer to speak her mind. Asked point-blank if her dad would run for president in 1980, Susan Ford responded, "No, my mom would divorce him. You can't be divorced and run for president at the same time."

In Ford's mind, the decision hadn't been made yet, but that didn't mean the decision hadn't been made—by Betty.

A Christian, a Jew, and a Muslim Walk into a Bar . . .

In the middle of September, Ford felt a twinge of yearning for the Oval Office and its powers. President Carter had invited Egyptian President

Anwar Sadat and Israeli Prime Minister Menachem Begin to meet him at Camp David. Carter was putting his presidency on the line, gambling that he could broker a peace between the two enemies. The three leaders were in Ford's element: the kind of high-level, high-stakes, internationally momentous occasion that he had been at the center of in Vladivostok and Helsinki.

There was very little news coming out of Camp David, and Ford understood why: news leaks could destroy whatever progress was being made. Still, he was profoundly curious. And when the meeting, scheduled for three days, stretched into four days, five days, then a week, Ford knew that although there was no news coming out of Camp David, news was certainly being made there.

On Sunday, September 17, 1978, the three men—Carter, Sadat, and Begin—boarded Marine 1. After twelve exasperating, turbulent days at the rustic retreat, they were bound for the White House. On the helicopter, they made a single phone call—to former president Ford. They wanted him to be the first to know that they had reached peace between Israel and Egypt, and they wanted to thank him for helping to lay the foundation for what came to be known as the Camp David Accords.

Ford said it was a great, historic moment and congratulated them on their achievement. Privately, however, he expressed misgivings. No American president could leach out centuries of bad blood in a couple of weeks. As extraordinary as this truce was between these two nations, it was an uneasy one. True conciliation in the Middle East would come at a very high price. Ford feared this would be a violent peace.

Bringing two fierce, strong-willed enemies to the table and brokering a peace between them takes patience, charm, quick thinking, and deception. I'm not talking about Begin and Sadat. A couple of other old foes were at it again, and within two years, the summer of 1980, they'd be sitting in the same room taking each other's measure—Ronald Reagan and Gerald Ford.

The Machiavelli Men

William Casey was present at the creation of the modern United States foreign intelligence apparatus. The Office of Strategic Services (OSS) was modeled after the British intelligence service. This predecessor of the CIA was formed in 1942, at President Roosevelt's behest, to coordinate espionage activities behind enemy lines during World War II. It was led by decorated soldier and legendary spymaster William "Wild Bill" Donovan. He filled the ranks of the fledgling Office by drawing on the branches of the US Armed Forces.

A successful New York corporate lawyer before the war, Casey now chafed behind a desk in the Navy Department. He offered himself up to Donovan, who signed him up and promptly sent him off to London. Casey proved himself to be adept at spy craft. Between dodging German incendiary bombs and V-2 rockets, he took the lead in organizing, arming, and directing the French resistance prior to D-Day. Following the success of the Allied invasion of the Continent, Donovan appointed him chief of secret intelligence for Europe. His mission: infiltrate Nazi Germany with OSS agents.

Fast-forward thirty-five years. July 14, 1980, was Gerald Ford's sixty-seventh birthday and, as it happened, first day of the Republican National Convention in Detroit. Ford was there to make a speech in support of the presumptive nominee, Ronald Reagan. Midafternoon, I received a call from Bill Casey who, along with longtime political operative Mike Deaver, was one of Reagan's closest advisors. Casey said Reagan wanted to extend birthday wishes to Ford.

Later that day, Ford and I made our way down some back stairs in the Detroit Plaza Hotel from the seventieth floor to the sixty-ninth where Reagan had his suite. After greeting Casey, who had served on the former president's Foreign Intelligence Advisory Board, Ford quickly went into an adjacent room where Reagan waited.

Casey and I sat on couches across from each other, the crack former intelligence officer looking more like rumpled TV detective Columbo than suave secret agent James Bond. Casey had a tendency to mumble, and when he spoke I politely asked him to repeat himself.

"He—" Casey said slowly, as if it were not his mumbling at issue, but my ability to comprehend, "—is going to ask him to be his running mate."

He being Ronald Reagan, *him* being Ford, and my first thought being *What the hell?*

Despite his daughter's conjecture that if he ran for president, it would be grounds for her mother to divorce him, Ford hadn't fully closed the door and thrown away the key until earlier that year, when Reagan had won enough delegates to lock up the nomination. In October 1979, after months of flirting with the possibility, Ford met with his inner circle in Rancho Mirage. They all agreed that he should make it clear that he was not running; many Republican donors were holding back their money in anticipation that Ford might enter the race, thus hurting other candidates.

Ford announced that he had made "a firm decision not to become an active candidate." Even then, he left the door open a crack: *an active candidate* being the key phrase. He would not seek the nomination, but if the nomination should seek him, that was a different story. If the convention were deadlocked, well, he would not refuse a draft.

President Carter, meanwhile, was facing political fire from his left flank as Ted Kennedy made a run at the Democratic nomination. Then, on November 4, 1979, a mob of Iranian students stormed the United States embassy in Tehran, taking fifty-two Americans hostage. The overthrown Shah of Iran was in a New York City hospital being treated for cancer, and the students demanded that, in exchange for releasing the Americans, he be returned to Tehran to face a trial and likely execution. The standoff dragged on into the campaign season.

Carter's presidency was imploding, the Camp David Accords had become a distant memory, and the path to the Oval Office seemed to run through Detroit for whomever the Republican nominee would be. For Ford, it was not to be. Reagan, who had been preparing the ground since his loss in 1976, stormed to the nomination, and Ford had accepted that he was not going to return to the White House. But now, here on the sixty-ninth floor of the Detroit Plaza Hotel, behind closed doors, those terms were being redefined.

"Bill," I said, "you just took a giant leap above my pay grade."

I would rarely presume to speak for Ford without first consulting with him, but in this case I couldn't hold back.

"He won't do it," I insisted.

"He'll do it," Bill mumbled confidently.

Later, back in his suite, Ford confirmed to me that Reagan had indeed popped the question.

"It would never work," he said. "But we should show some respect to his request. Who is here that can help with this?"

"Well," I said after a minute's thought, "Henry, Alan, and Jack."

Kissinger, Greenspan, and Marsh. I couldn't have come up with a more qualified or more loyal trio even if I had a year to think it over. Those three, along with me, would meet with Casey and Reagan's counsel (and future attorney general) Edwin Meese to consider the viability of a Reagan/Ford ticket. It took about three seconds for word to leak that such a dream ticket was being considered.

Batman teaming with Superman. Godzilla teaming with King Kong. Ford teaming with Reagan. The media went into hyper-mode, while the delegates on the convention floor went nuts. The Republicans believed they would steamroll over Carter and the Democrats and retake the presidency in a cakewalk.

But in love, war, and politics, what you see is not necessarily what is happening.

Our first meeting—the morning of Tuesday, July 15, thirty-six hours and counting to the scheduled announcement of Reagan's running mate—went smoothly, the first moves of a chess match, the two sides probing the opposition's defenses. The second meeting, that afternoon, took a more aggressive turn, pieces starting to fall.

We laid out Ford's conditions. He did not want to be a figurehead vice president—he would want a seat at the table, a voice in major decisions. And it was a package deal: Kissinger would stay on as secretary of state, and Greenspan would remain the chief advisor on economic policy. Meese and Casey were displeased with the proposal and pushed back. Reagan, they said, would not cede territory to Ford, turning the White House into a feudal state. Later, when he heard about their reluctance to accept his terms, Ford seemed both comfortable and relieved.

Still, we had one more meeting scheduled for the next day to see if a compromise could be hammered out. Meanwhile, the mood at the convention was frenzied, and journalists were on the hunt for stories. ABC reporter Barbara Walters had reached out to me to see if she could get an exclusive with Ford. I ran the idea by him, and he agreed to speak with her the next afternoon. But fate took a hand—in the person of Walter Cronkite.

Barbara was a star, but Walter was a legend. He was a titan of television journalism, and he got the exclusive. Ford thought having Cronkite do the interview would lend it more gravitas, and Barbara was left at the altar. It would not be the last time Ford—and I—would stand her up.

When the CBS Evening News came on the next day, July 16, it was as if someone had hit the mute button in the convention hall. Cronkite's interview with Ford had us all mesmerized. There was one question everyone wanted an answer to, and Cronkite asked it. Would Ford accept the nomination for vice president? It depends, Ford said and went on: He would only "go there with the belief that I will play a meaningful role across the board in the basic and crucial decisions that have to be made."

"A co-presidency," Cronkite remarked.

Ford did not disagree.

Reagan, however, watching in his suite, did.

With just hours to go before the announcement, we were still deep in negotiations with Reagan's team, when Meese abruptly stood up and cut the meeting short. The game apparently was over. We just didn't know who had won—or if there had been a different game being played all along.

I went back to Ford's suite to relate what had happened. He was in the bedroom in slacks and an undershirt, and before I could open my mouth, he said, "Bob, this just isn't going to work out. It's not fair to Betty. Go tell them I won't do it."

Again I headed down the back stairs to Reagan's suite. In the corridor I spotted a member of Reagan's staff ushering George H. W. Bush into another room. Fifteen minutes later, on the convention floor, Reagan introduced his running mate to the delegates: George Bush.

I had been in on everything every step of the way, attending every meeting, and I had no idea in hell what had happened over the last seventy-two hours. On the plane back to Vail, Ford looked pensively out the window and said, "Well, that was a pretty good convention, Bob. I gave a good speech, saw some good friends, and got a good man on the ticket."

Only then did I realize that there was one meeting I didn't attend—the one between Reagan and Ford when they met alone on the first day. Also, it occurred to me that both men got exactly what they wanted: a moderate on the ticket without three days of withering criticism from the right wing.

It had all been a magic trick. Create a diversion, make sure the audience is looking elsewhere when you pull the bunny—George Bush—out of your hat. The deal had Bill Casey's fingerprints all over it—deception and diversion being his stock-in-trade. If he could get the OSS into Nazi Germany, he could get a moderate past the media and onto the Republican presidential ticket.

The Reagans would go on to victory in November. They got what they wanted: the White House. We got to go home.

Reaping the Whirlwind

Two days later, on October 6, in a different desert on a different continent, a darker drama played out. As a military parade in Cairo marched
past the reviewing stand, four uniformed soldiers leaped out of one of the
troop trucks, tossing grenades and firing their AK-47s into the gallery.
The militants found their mark. Like Ronald Reagan, they got what they
wanted—Egyptian President Anwar Sadat was dead.

A Woman of Substance

Jerry had given up drinking, and now he gave up politics—eschewing both
for Betty. I have no doubt that leaving alcohol and Washington behind
added years to his life.

During her time as a politician's wife, Betty struggled with regret,
pondering the dreams she had failed to realize—a career as a model or
dancer on the New York stage. But fate, karma, chance—call it what you
will—moved her in a different direction. Her accomplishments would lie
elsewhere. What Betty Ford did was save lives—first, when she brought
breast cancer out of its dark, leprous corner, and now with her revelations
about her battles with chemical dependency. She would lead the way in
bringing that disease to light, as well.

On a Sunday morning early in October 1981, Betty dug a shovel into
the desert sand of Rancho Mirage, breaking ground on what would
become the Betty Ford Center, a nonprofit, residential treatment facility
for individuals suffering from substance abuse. In my role as the former
president's chief of staff, I took the lead in establishing his library,
the presidential museum, and this lasting legacy for the first lady. Betty
had found her stage after all.

7

State of the Union

Three Presidents and a Funeral

As the funeral procession made its way to the Unknown Soldier Memorial, where Sadat was to be buried, we slowly walked past the reviewing stand, the site of his assassination. His blood, intermingled with that of the ten others killed and twenty-eight wounded nine days before, still stained the marble. A bas-relief on the front of the stand depicted an ancient Egyptian army, on horseback and on foot, armed with shields and spears.

Anwar Sadat's political life was rooted in and shaped by violence. From a very early age, he detested the British occupiers of Egypt. As a young man he enlisted in the Egyptian army, convinced that the only hope for independence from Great Britain was the military. He plotted with like-minded officers—members of the Free Officers Association—the assassinations of British officials and of Egyptian leaders whom they viewed as British puppets. The two men Sadat most admired as a young man were Adolf Hitler and Mahatma Gandhi—not coincidentally, each, in his own way, a powerful enemy of Great Britain.

After the assassination of a British sympathizer, Sadat was arrested as an Islamic terrorist and put into solitary confinement. With no daylight and no bed for a year, and with only a copy of the Koran for company, Sadat's view of the world began to evolve. His conception of power, politics, and the best way to achieve Egyptian independence grew more sophisticated and nuanced. Terrorism, he concluded, led only to more terrorism. That kind of violence, often aimed at civilians, he reasoned, was the enemy of freedom and of a free people.

Sadat's beliefs continued to evolve after his release from prison, in no small part due to his marriage to the smart, beautiful Jehan Safwat Raouf. She gave him both a family and an even deeper conviction that the acquisition of power through the murder of innocents was, by definition, corrupt.

Still, convinced that the military was the key to Egyptian independence, Sadat reenlisted in the army and rejoined the Free Officers Association. Many of its members, including its leader, Gamal Abdel Nasser, urged an escalation of terrorist acts. Sadat argued for a revolution from within—seize control of the institutions of power, he argued, and we will ultimately control the power itself. Knowing that the world would be watching, Nasser came around to Sadat's point of view.

In 1952, the Free Officers Association, together with sympathizers throughout the military and police, executed a successful coup d'état. They overthrew the pro-British Egyptian monarchy and exiled King Farouk to Europe, convincing the British that their time in Cairo was over. At the beginning of the coup, the military seized a radio station to announce the coming action.

I assure the Egyptian people that the entire army today has become capable of operating in the national interest and under the rule of the constitution apart from any interests of its own. I take this opportunity to request that the people never permit any traitors to take refuge in deeds of destruction or violence because these are not in the interest of Egypt. Should anyone behave in such ways, he will be dealt with forcefully in a manner such as has not been seen before and his deeds will meet immediately the reward for treason. The army will take charge with the assistance of the police. I assure our foreign brothers that their interests, their souls, and their property are safe, and that the army considers itself responsible for them. May God grant us success.

The voice Egypt heard was that of a young officer, Anwar Sadat. Cheering mobs filled the streets.

Twenty years later, Sadat would become president of Egypt. Thirty years later, in one of the sad ironies of the twentieth century, Islamic extremists within his own army assassinated him.

Hat Trick

Heads of state from around the world made arrangements to attend Sadat's funeral. In Washington, however, President Reagan's brain trust was concerned about his safety. The situation in Cairo remained volatile, and if the Egyptian army couldn't be trusted to protect its own president, how could they be entrusted with Reagan's life?

Secretary of State Al Haig came up with a solution: a hat trick, as he called it. Send the three living former presidents—Richard Nixon, Gerald Ford, and Jimmy Carter—in Reagan's place.

At first, Carter resisted the idea. Not only was he still stinging from his loss to Reagan a year before, he also considered it an act of cowardice by the sitting president to stay back in Washington. Carter preferred to attend the funeral as a private citizen, as he considered Sadat to have been a close friend. Each of the three former presidents felt a personal relationship with and a respect for Sadat. Carter was pressured and finally persuaded to join the official American delegation.

Nixon, on the other hand, leaped at the opportunity. He was eager to rebuild his image on the national and international stage, and the funeral could be his ticket back to respectability.

Ford, uncharacteristically, played Hamlet, torn between family and country. Betty and the kids urged him not to accept the invitation. He had already survived two assassination attempts; to risk a third, they said, would be tempting fate. But the president had asked him to participate, and nothing if not loyal to his country, Ford agreed to join the others.

On Thursday, October 8, two days after Sadat's assassination, three Air Force jets touched down, one after the other, at Andrews Air Force Base in Maryland, each carrying a former president. I accompanied Ford, and the next several days would prove to be some of the most arduous, hectic, and intriguing in my life. Also present and just as apprehensive was Joe Canzeri, a former Rockefeller staffer. The two of us were supposed to take care of everything without having any idea of what was happening next.

The first quandary came as the three men approached Marine One, the helicopter that would take them to the White House to meet Reagan. It was a question of protocol. Who should be the first to board? Protocol is always based on precedent, but in this case there was none. Interestingly, it was Nixon who came up with the solution. He suggested that whoever had most recently left office would be the senior member of the delegation. Thus Carter boarded first, followed by Ford, then Nixon. There was some tension and unease among these lofty passengers, and Ford attempted to mitigate it.

"At least for this trip, why don't we just make it Dick, Jimmy, and Jerry?" he quipped.

All agreed to the informality. The rest of the entourage, including me, did not have that luxury. And this was one of the very rare occasions when saying *Mr. President* could cause not one, but three heads to turn.

Marine One chopped across the capital city's sky at dusk, the district's monuments casting long soft shadows across the streets and parks. It landed on the South Lawn of the White House as the day faded away. Washington may well be a swamp, but in the right light, it is a beautiful one.

Never before had four presidents been in the executive mansion at the same time. Considering that future president Vice President George H. W. Bush was also in attendance, there was a full quarter century of American executive power represented in the Blue Room that evening. An extraordinary, if somber, moment. But there were some light moments, as when they all raised a glass—in Nixon's case a coffee cup—in a toast to each other. Reagan and Carter had punch, Ford a club soda.

After about a half hour, the four men in gray flannel suits headed back out to the South Lawn, accompanied by Nancy Reagan in red and Rosalynn Carter, the only first lady to make the trip to Egypt, in green.

"There are moments in history," Reagan said, "when the martyrdom of a single life can symbolize all that is wrong with an age and all that is right with humanity."

Say what you want about Reagan, he had a way with words. And with that we reboarded Marine One for the ride back to Andrews.

As the helicopter rose into the night, Nixon turned to the others and said, "I kind of like that house down there. Don't you?"

Neither Ford nor Carter responded. If they had answered, however, I'm quite sure that they all would have answered *yes*.

Who's in Charge Here?

Self-importance is not in short supply in Washington. But in a town of monumental egos, some still find ways to rise above the rest.

In March 1981, seven months before the three presidents set off for Cairo, John Hinckley Jr. attempted to assassinate President Reagan. In so doing he had hoped to impress the actress Jodie Foster, with whom he had been obsessed since seeing her play the underage prostitute in the movie *Taxi Driver*. Hinckley accomplished neither. He wounded Reagan, a bullet ricocheting off the presidential limousine into his chest, and whatever impression he made on Jodie Foster was a negative one. He did, however, inadvertently succeed in setting off a bit of constitutional confusion.

Back in the White House, as Reagan was rushed to the hospital, Secretary of State Alexander Haig stood before the cameras to assure the country that he was "in charge." Which, of course, he wasn't. Vice President Bush and Speaker of the House Tip O'Neill were both alive and well and ahead of the secretary of state in the line of succession to the presidency.

Now, on this aircraft formerly known as Air Force One (Reagan had a newer, sleeker model), Haig once again exposed his presidential aspirations. The spacious forward cabin, which Nixon, Ford, and Carter had all enjoyed during their respective presidencies, now housed the official head of the delegation to Sadat's funeral, Secretary of State Alexander Haig. The three presidents, along with various other dignitaries, congressmen, and guests—Kissinger and musician Stevie Wonder among them—were relegated to an aft section. As Rosalynn Carter remarked, they were all flying coach to the Middle East.

The mood on the flight was tense. Every member of the delegation had been given a classified report on the political dangers in Egypt following Sadat's assassination, and that exacerbated the tension. What exactly were we flying into? Our security in Cairo would be provided, in large part, by the very same army out of which Sadat's assassins had risen.

Adding to the strain, there was a noticeable chill between the three presidents. Some of it was the history between them. Ford and Nixon had Watergate hanging over them, Ford feeling that Nixon had lied to him and then later failed to take full responsibility after receiving the pardon. Ford and Carter had fought a bitter campaign in 1976, and some of that bitterness lingered. As for Carter and Nixon, they simply did not like each other.

Once again, it was Nixon who broke the ice. For such a divisive figure, he had a gift for finding common ground with those opposed to him. He had a lot of practice. He complimented Mrs. Carter on her dress, and then shared with her the challenges he and his wife were having in buying a house in New Jersey. Despite herself, she started to warm to him. He then told Ford and Carter that he believed they had both served the country well, and before you knew it, the three of them were thick as thieves.

They talked about writing their memoirs, transitioning from the White House to private life, and raising money to fund the construction of their presidential libraries. China, the Soviet Union, Saudi Arabia, and the situation in the Middle East were all up for discussion. They shared their views about power and about the people in Washington who wielded it. The flight made for a marvelous mash-up of history, insight, and gossip. Having the participation and expertise of Kissinger and Scowcroft on board contributed to accurate and detailed presidential recollections.

By the time the retired Air Force One touched down in Cairo, we were all exhausted, exhilarated, and on edge about what awaited us on the ground. The three presidents climbed into three armor-plated limousines with Washington plates, flown over from DC for the occasion.

Collateral Damage

Two hundred thirty miles to the south, in the Egyptian city of Asyut, forty people were reported killed in clashes between Islamic fundamentalists and the police. The streets of Cairo, however, were eerily quiet, deserted except for the security forces posted on virtually every corner or speeding around the city in trucks. Despite the ubiquitous security—or perhaps because of it—the US Secret Service agents were antsy, all eyes and ears, scanning rooftops and peering down dusty alleyways.

After a stop for a brief rest at our hotel in downtown Cairo, the entourage continued on to an official meeting with Sadat's successor, Vice President Hosni Mubarak. With that out of the way, the motorcade then continued, crossing the Nile and driving some three miles south to Giza, on the west bank, near the Giza Plateau, site of the Great Pyramid and Great Sphinx.

But the presidents were not here to sightsee. The limos pulled up in front of a modest, well-appointed house with a pleasant garden out front. The residence was surrounded by soldiers and, a bit farther out, by members of the press. The three presidents exited their cars and followed a short footpath through the garden into the front entrance of the home.

Jehan Sadat, Anwar's widow, sat on a couch in a sun-filled room off the main hall. She appeared composed; still, the grief was etched on her face. We tend to forget that great public tragedies are also great private ones. Egypt may have lost its heroic leader, but children had also lost a father, and a wife her husband. They, too, are victims of the assassins' bullets.

She was now surrounded by three grim-faced presidents, as Nixon, Ford, and Carter went in to sit with her and offer their condolences. Sadat had worked with each of them on major problems and policies in the Middle East. I stayed just outside in the hall, with a view into the room. I could see that Ford was growing emotional, grasping his hands together. I turned away, feeling as though I was intruding on a private moment. I looked out the front door, through the garden, into the street, and saw a familiar face.

Barbara Walters had broken away from the press and talked her way past the security detail. She smelled an exclusive story and wasn't going to let a few soldiers holding rifles with fixed bayonets keep her from it. Barbara beckoned for me to come out and talk to her.

"Bob," she said, "can you get them to stop on their way out, just for a moment, just a few words. I'm sure the world would like to know what they have to say."

"The Egyptian government has asked them not to speak to the press," I said.

"One minute, Bob, that's all I'm asking. Don't worry, I'll smooth it over with the Egyptians."

I wasn't very good at saying "no" to most women, and I don't think anyone was very good at saying "no" to Barbara.

"I'll tell them you are here," I promised her.

The three presidents stood to say their goodbyes to Jehan. I hurried back into the hall to intercept them before they reached the door. I knew they'd be in no mood to dawdle, so I put on my best, fast-talking New York accent, and said:

"Mr. Presidents,"—plural—"Barbara Walters is outside asking you to stop for a second, to say something to the American people."

Each of them responded in character:

Ford, a man of few words, said, "Okay, Bob."

Carter, a man of just a few more words, responded, "I understand, Bob, I understand. Barbara Walters sees an angle for her story: *American presidents comfort the widow.*"

And Nixon, always on the defensive with the press, shook his head. "Damn it, the press goes too far. Too far!"

All three presidents walked outside and, without so much as a glance in Barbara's direction, disappeared into their limos. I shrugged at her and headed for the motorcade. First at the convention in Detroit, and now again at the widow's home in Cairo—I seemed destined to disappoint Barbara Walters. That bothered me because I liked Barbara. She was tough, bright, and relentless. She had little tolerance for—and no fear of—the male species.

The Road to Paradise

The next morning, Saturday, October 11, the headline in the Cairo paper read: THE PYRAMID IS GONE. Under a hot desert sun, Egypt buried its president.

The three American presidents, together with the leaders of more than eighty countries, waited under a large multicolored tent on the parade ground—the very same ground on which Sadat's assassins had, just a few days before, successfully staged their savage attack. The mood was surreal.

No one had briefed us. We were in the dark about the organization, timing, and security at the funeral. We saw it unfold as it happened. Leaders of state and former leaders of state are not used to being kept in the dark.

The large congregation marched about a quarter of a mile to take part in the solemn event. Soldiers on horseback patrolled the surrounding dunes. Heavy machine guns mounted on jeeps stood on either side of the reviewing stand. Over twenty Secret Service agents guarded our delegation, carrying automatic weapons hidden in plastic cases.

After what seemed an eternity in the oppressive heat, distant drums began to play, announcing the imminent arrival of Sadat's body. A helicopter slowly approached, circled overhead, then descended, kicking up a swirl of white dust. The casket, under the red, white, and black flag of Egypt, was carried out of the helicopter and placed onto a horse-drawn caisson. The drums drew nearer. Mrs. Sadat, in black, took a seat just a few feet from where her husband had been killed.

A soldier on an Arabian horse led the procession, followed by musicians and lancers on horseback. There were soldiers, marching units from military academies, and more soldiers flanking the coffin. The dignitaries and their delegations followed—a jumble of figures in military uniforms, flowing robes, and dark business suits making their way across the parade ground.

Ford walked alongside Prime Minister Begin of Israel, then former French president Valery Giscard d'Estaing, Carter, Nixon, and Kissinger. They had all been issued heavy bulletproof vests. Joe Canzeri and I, walking several rows behind them, had not. The thinking being, I suppose, that executive assistants were rarely targeted for assassination. It was small comfort.

At one point the whole procession drew to a sudden halt because of gunfire in the distance. After a few discomforting minutes, word came that a group of Egyptian civilians, kept at a distance from the ceremony, had broken through the lines of security and warning shots had been fired to stop them. They had simply wanted a closer look at their slain leader. We could hear them calling out, "God is great!" and "Sadat to paradise!"

Unfortunately, this road to paradise was stained with blood, Sadat buried some three hundred and fifty feet from where he had been murdered. In the Middle East, the price of paradise is extremely high.

We didn't stay to see Sadat undertake the final leg of that journey. Our security contingent whisked us out of the procession, and we were in the air before the coffin was in the ground. There was, however, one glitch in our flight plan.

Nixon.

The press pool for the flight back consisted of three journalists: Steve Bell of ABC News, Haynes Johnson from the *Washington Post*, and UPI's Jim Anderson. While the plane was still on the ground, Bell came to me and asked if they could get an interview with the three presidents. Haig was staying on in Cairo for talks with Mubarak, so the presidents were in the forward cabin. I went up to see if they would agree to some face time with the press.

I came back with their answer.

"I've got good news and bad news," I said to the newsmen. "They'll sit for an interview—but there's only two of them here."

Without me saying another word, Haynes Johnson, who had been around the political block a few times, especially with Watergate, growled, "Goddamn it, what did Nixon do now!?"

Nixon, it turned out, was just being Nixon—as calculating and secretive as ever—arranging to fly on his own to Jeddah, Saudi Arabia, for talks with the Saudi leaders. He had not told anyone in the delegation of his plans. When Ford found out, he leaned over to Kissinger and said:

"Can you believe that damn stunt?"

Obviously, Kissinger knew better than anyone what Nixon was capable of doing, both by design and with deception.

That was one of the few times I ever heard Ford swear with conviction, albeit in a somewhat muted manner.

The Seven-Year Itch

From the time I signed up to join the army, the government had taken good care of me. It had given me the opportunity to learn about leadership and management and to develop and enhance my skills as a writer. The government had provided me with three square meals a day, a roof over my head, a master's degree from Syracuse University, and finally, and most fortunately, entrée to the White House to work with the Fords and travel the world.

But now, seven years after first walking into the Oval Office to meet Ford, it was time for me to move on—time for me to get off the government dime and go out into the real world to make some real money. The Sadat funeral marked the end of my government service.

My relationship with the Ford family remained as strong as ever, and they would continue to be an integral part of my life. I joined them for golf tournaments and special occasions, spent vacations with them, and often traveled with the former president. But I was going out on my own now, leaving the nest that the Fords had made for me. I had work to do and places to go.

Epilogue

I put out a shingle, Barrett and Associates, and drawing on my experience in fundraising, hired myself out as a consultant, focusing on political campaigns and lobbying. I had just turned fifty and signed up for my third marriage when, at long last, my ship came in—more of a boat, really, but a bigger boat than I was used to.

UST, formerly United States Tobacco, dominated the smokeless tobacco market through its Skoal and Copenhagen brands. During his two decades leading the company, chairman and CEO Lou Bantle had overseen a billion-dollar increase in sales. Also involved in philanthropy and Republican politics, Bantle, a quiet but truly outstanding gentleman, had developed a friendship with Ford. I came to know him as a golfing partner in Vail.

We had common ground. We had both attended Syracuse University and had both served in a wartime military—me in Vietnam, Bantle as a captain in the US Marine Corps during the Korean War. He also liked my connections in Washington and asked me to serve on UST's board of directors. Not long after that, he decided to bring me inside the company as a senior vice president.

There was more to UST than smokeless tobacco. In addition to my role as senior vice president, I was also named president of a couple of subsidiary companies: Stimson Lane Vineyards and Estates, with wineries in California and Washington State, and a small production house, Cabin Fever Entertainment. My primary responsibility was government relations, flying back and forth to Washington on one of the company's three jets. Because of my background, I was also the primary organizer of many of UST's largest events—golf tournaments, company dinners, meetings with senators and other major players.

Through it all, I continued to spend as much time as possible with my adopted Ford family. It was in the mid- to late-1990s that the president had a heart-to-heart talk with his only daughter, Susan.

"Now, Susan," he said in his stiff, paternal, Midwestern way, "I really don't think you should be smoking."

Susan, who inherited her mother's outspokenness, snapped, "I'll quit smoking cigarettes when you give up your pipes."

He called in Penny Circle, his assistant at the time.

"I need you to gather up all of my pipes," he said.

"All of them?"

"Every last one. Box them up for me."

Over the years he had accumulated quite a collection—dozens and dozens, gifts from many notable people from all over the world. He told her to ship them to the Ford Presidential Museum where, as far as I know, they still are today. Gerald Ford would never ask anyone to do something he wasn't willing to do himself.

Every year, it seemed, either Ford was presenting Kissinger with an award or Kissinger was presenting one to Ford. This particular year, it was Ford's turn to do the honors—at the annual awards ceremony of the American Jewish Congress in New York. Ford had asked me to accompany him on the trip to the East Coast, and this was the first stop—a black-tie affair at the St. Regis Hotel. He would make a speech, hand over the hardware, have a nice dinner, and stay overnight at the hotel, and then the next morning we were scheduled to head up to visit the Rockefeller family at their estate in Westchester.

The event also served as a fundraiser for the organization, and a friend of Ford's back in Palm Springs had arranged for a New York businessman, Joe Parker was his name, to buy a table—ten dinners at $1,000 a pop.

I went over to thank him for coming, for contributing to this worthy cause and so on and so forth. I said all the right things, but my mind—and my eye—was wandering. Seated at the table, in a purple and blue gown, was an absolutely stunning woman. All I cared about was the smile she gave me when I walked up to the table.

Joe invited me to join them, but of course I couldn't. My job was to look after Ford, make sure he got through this ceremony, and then get him up to his room afterward.

As far as I was concerned, the event couldn't end fast enough. Finally, dinners consumed, speeches spoken, and the awards handed out, I took Kissinger and the president up to Ford's suite and hurried back downstairs. My prayers were answered. The Parker party was still there, and I joined it.

I dropped the line that has proved so useful to me so many times:

"Would you like to meet the president?"

She said "sure"—a president makes a damn good wingman—and up we went.

The evening became instantly enhanced.

In the president's suite, Ford knew exactly what I was up to, but he was as gracious as ever, making small talk and shaking her hand. But then Kissinger took her hand, and I wasn't sure if he was ever going to let it go. Kissinger may not have had movie-star good looks, but he's suave, funny, and as charming as Charles Boyer. And as everyone knows, he has an eye for beautiful women.

I love Henry. He's like a brilliant, mischievous uncle you never get enough time with. I'm sure he wouldn't have done a thing. But I wasn't taking any chances that this beautiful woman would dump me to spend more time with him.

"Well, we better get going," I said after a quick cocktail and made a break for it—a quick escape that led to a memorable night. I overslept the next morning, waking up at eight. An hour too late for my departure with Ford.

The former president was sitting in a small private jet on the tarmac at LaGuardia. It was scheduled to take off for Westchester Airport—at eight. I picked up the phone and called the Secret Service agents assigned to him.

"Bob, where are you?"

"It doesn't matter where I am," I answered. "Get him up to the Rockefellers! I'll catch up later."

It's a fundamental rule of presidential life—whether the individual in question is a former president or not—you don't mess with his schedule.

I gave the woman a kiss on the cheek and double-timed it down to the street to catch a cab. I'd figure out my next move once I got to LaGuardia—maybe rent a car and drive up to Westchester. But I didn't have to. When I got to the airport, still in a black tie and tuxedo, Ford's puddle jumper was still sitting on the tarmac. I strode up to the Secret Service agent standing next to it, clearly waiting on me.

"What are you still doing here?"

"Don't get on my case," he said. "We all wanted to go. All of us except *him*. *He* wanted to wait."

Sheepishly, I climbed up into the plane. Ford was reading the *New York Times*. Hearing me, he lowered the newspaper just enough so I could see his eyes and the slow shake of his head. Then he raised the paper and went back to the news. Ford might have been a Boy Scout, but he knew that I was not. That I was still in black tie, the same outfit I had been in the night before, was a dead giveaway. He indulged me, secretly enjoying my misdeeds and misdemeanors.

The Indispensable Man

The news didn't come as a surprise. Still, it broke my heart. The day after Christmas, 2006, President Ford passed away. And a piece of me died that day as well. I loved the man, I loved his family, and I loved his world. Working for him in the White House and afterward was an invitation into the bubble—with unique access to politicians, journalists, and celebrities and a behind-the-scenes view of the world stage.

Thanks to Ford, I had the opportunity to form friendships with such extraordinary individuals as Dick Cheney, Brent Scowcroft, and Susan Ford; to meet, romance, and enjoy the company of beautiful women around the world; to send my mom a photo of me with the pope to put on her fridge. I have wined and dined with Clint Eastwood, golfed with Jack Nicklaus, talked history with Henry Kissinger (granted, a one-sided conversation), joked with Bill Murray, and shared the stage with Bob Hope. I didn't owe Ford my life, but I did owe him the life that I lived . . . thirty-two years in all.

I was one of the honorary pallbearers for the services in Washington. Among the speakers was the former president George H. W. Bush. He said of Ford:

> *Time and again he would step forward and keep his promise even when the dark clouds of political crisis gathered over America. As Americans, we generally eschew notions of the indispensable man, and yet during those traumatic times, few if any of our public leaders could have stepped into the breach and rekindled our national faith as did President Gerald R. Ford.*

Ford's death marked more than the end of one man's life. It marked the end of an era. The great leaders who had emerged out of the Second World War, in America—Eisenhower, Kennedy, Johnson, and Ford—and around the world—Thatcher, Brandt, Indira Gandhi of India, and, of course, Sadat in Egypt—were gone. The torch had been passed to a newer, younger generation of leaders, and some would be burned by it.

In Colorado, Vail is considered Republican country, while Aspen is traditionally a Democratic resort. In 1993, following the first year of his presidency, Bill Clinton and his wife, Hillary, paid a visit to Ford in Vail. Clinton had two objectives: play golf with Jack Nicklaus and demonstrate his willingness to work with the Republicans. Following their visit, I went to lunch with Ford, and, over soup and sandwiches, I asked his opinion of the Clintons.

"Well, Bob," he said, "I don't know what's at the man's core, but you tell all our Republican friends not to underestimate this guy. He could sell three-day-old ice to Eskimos." Ford paused, took a bite, then added, "But you know what? Hillary, she's the strong one."

The Great Liberator

"Hi. I'm Betty Ford, and I'm an alcoholic."

In the 1970s, the former first lady brought breast cancer out of the shadows. A decade later, she did the same for alcoholism. Just as her husband had stepped up to bring the country back to health from the sickness of Watergate, Betty had courageously spoken those words in public—the beginning of an intervention that would save thousands of lives across the country. Five years after burying her husband, I traveled to Grand Rapids to help America lay her to rest.

Presidential historian and former director of the Ford museum Richard Norton Smith spoke at the service:

> More than a liberated woman, Betty Ford was herself a great liberator. Perhaps her greatest accomplishment was to help liberate us all from the crippling limits of labels.

I will always think of her dancing on the tables in the White House, acting as matchmaker between me and her interpreter in the Soviet Union, and at an improvised volleyball game in Vail. She jumped to hit the ball, and her breast prosthesis slipped. Brent Scowcroft, also in the game, and a consummate gentleman, stepped over to shield her from embarrassment. But she didn't need shielding; she only needed to laugh. That was Betty Ford: living, flirting, dazzling, dancing on the tables, and laughing in the face of cancer. On Thursday, July 14, 2011, she was buried alongside her husband at the Gerald R. Ford Presidential Museum.

Gerald Ford was never elected to America's highest office, but he was the most decent, honest man to serve as president in my adult lifetime. He inspired loyalty and dedication everywhere he went—people around him did everything they could *not* to let him down. Every member of his staff loved serving under him—he fostered a healthy, positive atmosphere that made work a joy. All I had to do was talk with those who remained in Ford's White House after serving in Nixon's to know the significant difference Ford made in improving their lives.

Some people, as they get older, wish that they could hit the reset button and recapture their youth. I'm not one of them. I wouldn't trade in the life I've had for anything—certainly not for a newer model. The incredible opportunities I have had from the age of thirty-five, as a young, inconsequential army major, until today, I owe to Jerry, Betty, and the Ford family.

I will remain forever grateful.

Acknowledgments

Fifth and Final

At least no one can say I was a quitter. My fifth wife, Eleanor, stayed with me through thick and thin, and there was a lot of both. She took care of me through my illness and was instrumental in getting me focused on completing this book. I'm sure she knows I'll miss her love and companionship.

So, as you know now, I was married five times . . . Big deal. The only consistent love in my life has been my two children, Nils and Kristy. No father could be prouder of his kids. They are by far my greatest achievement.

Show Business

I left UST in 2001, but some of the friendships I formed during my time there—especially in my work with Cabin Fever—are some of the most durable and compelling in my life. I turned sixty-five the same year I married my fourth wife, Dominique, and my birthday was marked by a spectacular affair at the same country club where the wedding had taken place. The event was written, directed, and produced—from hors d'oeuvres to the music—by Robert (Bobby) Halmi Jr.

Bobby Halmi Jr. and his dad, Robert Halmi Sr., are two of the most prolific and talented individuals in the entertainment business you've probably never heard of. Halmi Sr., born in Hungary, veteran of the underground wars against both the Nazis and the Communists, came to America with five dollars in his pocket and turned it, with his son Bobby's help, into a multi-billion-dollar moviemaking machine. The father came up with the creative ideas, the son with the creative financing.

In the summer of 2014, the elder Halmi died at the age of ninety-one, having enjoyed enough experiences to fill half a dozen lifetimes. The younger Halmi, whom I first met in my capacity as president of Cabin Fever, has become one of my closest friends. We have in common a love of golf, a fearlessness that borders on recklessness, and a penchant for serial marriage.

If Bobby doesn't like you—if he senses that you are pretentious or narcissistic—he will walk away, wanting nothing to do with you; diplomacy is not his strong suit. On the other hand, if he takes to you, you won't find a truer or more generous friend—or a more competitive one.

We used to work together, putting on shows for various events and anniversaries at the club, and every time I came up with an idea, Bobby would double down and then triple down. We should get a band, I'd say—and he'd get an orchestra. Dancing girls, I'd suggest—and he'd bring in the Rockettes. I said once that a bagpiper would be nice—and we ended up with a team of twenty-five of them, accompanied by drummers, marching up the eighteenth fairway.

On the occasion of my sixty-fifth birthday, Bobby went all out. He made a video to show at the party, heading out to Vail with a film crew to talk to Ford, who had all these wonderful, gracious things to say about me.

What Bobby neglected to tell the former president was that the film wasn't exactly rated G. But it was certainly entertaining, seeing the old Boy Scout President Ford intercut with all these women jumping around in bikinis. But that's Bobby for you, the consummate impresario, the guy behind the curtain—the bigger the show, the bigger the deal, the more he likes it.

I've had many golf buddies and numerous drinking partners, but only a few foxhole friends. Halmi is one of those. It has nothing to do with money, power, or background. It has everything to do with trust, respect, and a healthy sense of humor.

Unsurprisingly, Bobby was enormously helpful in seeing that this book got written. I hope he knows how grateful I am.

Index